ENCOUNTERING THE SUPERNATURAL

Bruce Lindley

Foreword by James W. Goll

"ENCOUNTERING THE SUPERNATURAL"

by Bruce Lindley

3rd Edition - October 2025

Published by ARC Global: PO Box 3398 Helensvale QLD 4212 Australia

Originally Published in 2011

This book or parts thereof may not be reproduced in any form, stored in a retrieval system, or transmitted in any form by any means – electronic, mechanical, photocopy, recording or otherwise – without prior written permission of the publisher, except as provided by Australia copyright law.

All scripture quotations are from the New International Version 1984 of the Bible unless otherwise specified.

Scripture taken from the HOLY BIBLE, NEW INTERNATIONAL VERSION.

Copyright © 1973, 1978, 1984 by International Bible Society. Used by permission of Zondervan. All rights reserved.

Copyright © 2025 Bruce Lindley

Cover design by Rachel LeRoux

ISBN: 978-0-646-56249-0

Printed in Australia

Dedication

"Encounters in the Supernatural" is dedicated to my wonderful Heavenly Father who continues to open new levels of the supernatural for me through intimacy. Thank you, Father God!

I would also like to dedicate this book to the following people who have specifically shaped and guided my journey into encountering the supernatural:

Jack and Leonie Frewen-Lord who taught me how to experience the overflow of the Holy Spirit and how to pray for others to be healed.

Clark Taylor who showed me how to move in the power of the supernatural and function in spiritual gifts. Your example still impacts me today.

Tom Whiting, the Pentecostal pioneer in our city, for his consistent example of encountering the Holy Spirit and encouragement to me to do the same.

Che Ahn and my Harvest International Ministries family who pursue the supernatural river of His presence with passion purity and authority. Your fathering is never taken for granted.

Heidi Baker who challenged me to stop for the "one" and not be satisfied with anything less than supernatural transformation of people and nations.

Katherine Ruonala who challenged me by her example to press further into His heart for fresh supernatural encounters.

My precious wife Cheryl whose passion and intimacy with Jesus overwhelms me.

My wonderful children whose hunger for more of Him blesses me beyond words.

Acknowledgements

This book wouldn't have been possible without the support and help of Paul and Pamela Segneri, and their ongoing commitment, love and input into this project. Thank you. Have a great harvest in the supernatural.

Special thanks to Katherine and Tom Ruonala from New Day Ministries, for lending me their home to write this book and their ongoing love and support.

Contents

Foreword - James W. Goll.... p9

Introduction - Encountering The Supernatural.... p11

1 - How To Begin The Encounter Of The Supernatural. p15

2 - Naturally Supernatural.... p23

3 - Choosing To Step Into The Supernatural.... p41

4 - Building The Atmosphere For The Supernatural.... p53

5 - A Generation Of The Double Encounter.... p63

6 - The Power Of The Holy Spirit's Overflow.... p77

7 - Glory That Lasts.... p99

8 - Moving To The Next Level Of The Supernatural.... p115

9 - Your Supernatural Transformation.... p129

Appendix 1 - Healing Scriptures.... p141

Appendix 2 - Spiritual Gift Definitions.... p145

Endnotes.... p151

ARC Global Apostolic Community.... p155

Contact And Resource Details.... p157

Foreword by James W. Goll

Moving in the supernatural is an amazing way of life and a choice. It is a choice you will never regret but initially might fear. We each make many choices in our pilgrimage and maturity process in our relationship with our Father God, His Son, Jesus Christ and the third person of the godhead, the Holy Spirit. Supernatural encounters increase the more you choose to "let go of your own control" and "let Him have His way!"

Just by picking up this book you have already expressed interest in being more than a nominal believer. You are making a choice right now and expressing interest in going deeper in God and the things of God. You have a hunger for an authentic move of the Holy Spirit in your day, your generation. If you are like me, you honor the historic moves of God in the past – but there is something rising up within you that cries out for a visitation in your own time!

Well, if that is the case, then you have just picked up a tool in God that will equip you to trust in the Lord and lean not on your prior understanding! Supernatural encounters are your inheritance in Christ!

Bruce Lindley, in this book, Encountering the Supernatural, has delivered right into your hands a stick of dynamite. Bruce equally loves the Word of God and the activity of the Holy Spirit. He exhibits the wedding of the School of the Word and the School of the Spirit in his life and ministry. Bruce will incite you to live in the Spirit and move into your next level! You will be taught how to move from encounters into transformation.

As the founder of Encounters Network, an author of numerous books and international travels, I have spent years cultivating a culture where the Holy Spirit will dwell. With this in mind, it is my joy to endorse the life and ministry and now the exciting book of my fellow Harvest International Ministry leader, Bruce Lindley. Fasten your seat belt, because you are about to go on the ride of a life time filled with adventure, constant new lessons, and encounters with a supernatural God!

James W. Goll

Encounters Network • Prayer Storm • Compassion Acts
Author of The Seer, Dream Language, God Encounters, The Lost Art of Intercession and many others.

Introduction

ENCOUNTERING THE SUPERNATURAL

Encountering the supernatural is powerful and exciting. It is also very real. Yet in western society this is looked on skeptically. Everything is viewed through the filter of logic. To an unspiritual mind the supernatural is illogical and therefore rejected.

Sociologists studying western culture call it the "excluded middle". We exclude the supernatural out of our western mindsets. That doesn't mean it doesn't exist!

On the other hand, the youth culture of today has no problem with the supernatural. This is evidenced by their embrace of the Harry Potter and the Twilight series of books and movies that dominate their focus and the media. Some of the most popular computer games have the supernatural as its base! The rise in the popularity of the New Age with people of all ages in our culture tells us that there is a genuine hunger for the supernatural.

Inherent in western culture is the desire to control and explain everything. This is the complete opposite mindset needed to encounter the supernatural.

The supernatural is very important for you and me. It is the only way that you will discover your true meaning and purpose in life. It will cause your spiritual intuition, your creativity and the power of your conscience to be awakened! Most importantly it will introduce you to the son of God who is the true source of spiritual power! So within this context the supernatural is very logical and does make sense. We just need to open ourselves up to it's amazing possibilities.

I wrote this introduction as I was travelling in Cambodia to visit a Christian humanitarian project rescuing children from sex slavery and trafficking on the Thai Cambodian border. As I addressed the large staff of the Cambodian Hope Organization on the first day I was there, the significance of this timing was not lost on me!

When I was eighteen years old, I made a decision that revolutionized my life and caused me to begin an encounter with the supernatural. I choose to surrender my life to Jesus Christ and ask him to take over my life so I would live for Him. What happened to me next was extraordinary. My life was turned right side up and my heart was captured by the love of Jesus! The joy and the peace I suddenly experienced overflowed to all those around me. Some of family were so impacted that they also became Christ ones! Suddenly the supernatural realm came alive to me. I learnt to listen to inner voice of heaven in my spirit. And when I did those things, extraordinary things happened. Lives were changed around me. But there was a hunger inside me for more!

INTRODUCTION

At that time I read a book called 'Anointed for Burial' by Todd and DeAnn Burke

(1). It was true story of a supernatural encounters by Christians in Cambodia just before the nation was taken over by the oppressive regime of Pol Pot and the Khmer Rouge. The world saw the horrendous stories of the Cambodian genocide in the media but that was only half the story. 'Anointed for Burial' told the other half!

I read how amazing supernatural miracles started to happen to the Christian believers in the midst of the killing fields and atrocities! Whole villages were bombarded yet time and time again the only houses not destroyed was the homes where the believers lived. They saw dramatic healings when they prayed for others who had been injured and even the dead bought back to life. Their lives were spared repeatedly and were inexplicably released from prison even after they had been arrested for their beliefs. Unexplainable multiplication of food often took place. As the result of these supernatural occurrences hundreds of people became Christians even though it meant they would be persecuted by the communist regime! The miracles of the Bible had come alive for the Christians in Cambodia.

Their story captured my heart and provoked me to desire to encounter the supernatural even more in my life.

Today most of my life decisions are made through the inspiration from spiritual dreams that I experience most nights. They are not abstract but specific and rational. As well, I often 'see' into the supernatural realm when I am praying for people and give them keys that unlock their lives. I have learnt to pull back the curtain of the natural and step into the supernatural easily!

'Encountering the Supernatural' will take you on a journey. From the beginning you will learn how to be naturally supernatural. You will be shown how to step into the supernatural daily! And you will learn how to build an overt atmosphere of the supernatural around your life that you take with you every day.

But that is not all!

This is an incredible time to be alive right now! The supernatural truths that took our spiritual fathers' generations to discover and step into are available to you today! Right here right now! There are no limitations. They are yours to experience and live in.

If you are already encountering the supernatural in your life, this book will help you grow to a greater depth. You are about to go from your current level to the next!

Maybe you have begun to read this book because you are curious or even desire to encounter the supernatural! There is so much more for you. Put aside your filters as you read this book.

Get ready to encounter a whole new realm of the supernatural!

CHAPTER 1

How To Begin The Journey Into The Supernatural

Oprah Winfrey's visit to Australia was nothing short of amazing in 2010. It was of epic proportions. She paid for over 300 guests in the audience of her show to travel with her from the USA to "down under". The response from Australian public was even more amazing with huge crowds waiting for hours to see her. She performed two shows to an audience of 5000 people on the steps of the Sydney Opera House. The tickets were only available on a ballot system with many people travelling from all over Australia to attend. It was nothing short of a phenomenon!

Why was Oprah so popular?

Cynics would say it is like a cult of personality, and some have even said that she has a messiah like influence on people.

But the most obvious answer is her generosity. She gave to her audience and staff in an amazing generous way.

But there is also another reason. Oprah is a hope giver.

She speaks and lives hope. She appreciates all those she meets in life. One of her quotable quotes is "nothing works for me unless it works for everybody"

What is she doing? Giving value to others to others by valuing them with her actions and words!

It some ways she is a type of Christian example, even though she doesn't believe in Jesus Christ as the only savior of humankind. In fact, she believes just the opposite! Oprah believes that humans have God within us and therefore we can save ourselves.

Nothing could be farther from the truth! This is completely contrary to the gospel of Jesus Christ! And it will not result in a lasting peace if you are truly desiring to live a supernatural life.

The Bible gives the true definition of the gospel in 1 Corinthians 15:3 when Paul says

> .....For what I received I passed on to you as of first importance: that Christ died for our sins according to the Scriptures, that he was buried, that he was raised on the third day according to the Scriptures..

So the gospel of Jesus the Christ is very different to the type of gospel that Oprah preaches. It does not discriminate. It will do for you what is has been done for millions of people over the last 2000 years.

The love of Jesus Christ sets your free! Jesus said it himself in John 8:32

> you will know the truth, and the truth will set you free.

What truth is he referring to? His!

Jesus said in John 14:6

> I am the way and the TRUTH and the life. No one comes to the Father except through me."

Like most people you may question truth to make sure it is real!

Then you are just like those you questioned Jesus too in John 8:34-36

> They answered him, "How can you say that we shall be set free?" Jesus replied, "I tell you, everyone who sins is a slave to sin. Now a slave has no permanent place in the family, but a son belongs to it forever. So if the Son sets you free, you will be free indeed.

Free from your sin and the burden of guilt! And free from the shame that you cannot set yourself free from. It is a love gift. A divine exchange!

We who are so undeserving are given the grace of love, acceptance and unconditional forgiveness by a savior who took our place!

God's word in Ephesians 2:8 tells you that you can never be good enough! There is nothing you can ever do to deserve God's love.

For it is by grace you have been saved, through faith— and this is not from yourselves, it is the gift of God— not by works, so that no one can boast.

Oprah and the new age teachers are wrong. This is not a self-help quest for spiritual peace or a journey into the supernatural that she or any other spiritual guide has the answer! This is the real thing!

Jesus is the only true way into the supernatural! He is the only true door that you enter it through!

So, you need to understand what has been done for you by him to do that.

Ephesians 2:13 says

> But now in Christ Jesus you who once were far away have been brought near by the blood of Christ.

Jesus has taken your place and done it for you!

He has made peace with God on your behalf! Verse 14 says

> For he himself is our peace, who has made the two groups one and has destroyed the barrier, the dividing wall of hostility..

Why?

Why would God do this? The only answer is His amazing grace and unconditional love for you and I!

Charles Wesley wrote in 1738 in the hymn "And Can It Be That I Should Gain" (1)

"Amazing love! How can it be,

that thou, my God, shouldst die for me?"

But wait it gets better!

"And can it be that I should gain an interest in the Savior's blood?

died He for me, who caused His pain— for me, who Him to death pursued?

Amazing love! How can it be,

that thou, my God, shouldst die for me?"

That is the good news of the gospel! It is freely given and can be freely received by you. It is your decision.

Why don't you do it now if you haven't ever done it before. It is not difficult. In fact that is the great deception of religion. To ask Jesus Christ to take control of your life is not hard at all. It just requires you to be honest with yourself and honest with God and to humbly ask him to take control of your life from now on. If you have never done that before here is a simple prayer that you can use that will help you do just that.

ADMIT – "Jesus I admit that I need you. I am self-centered and selfish, and I need a Savior."

Romans 3:23 put it this way

All have sinned and fall short of the glory of God

It is important to realize that you will never to good enough to save yourself. That is why you need a savior! But there is another important fact here. The glory of God is your way into the supernatural. So to begin your supernatural journey you need to regain the distance that you have fallen short. Jesus is the only way to do that. Ask him now.

ASK – "I ask that you forgive me for my all sins (pause a moment here and be specific). I ask that you come into my life and take control. I ask that you reveal your love to me."

God's word declares this over you today in 1 John 1:9

If we confess our sins, he is faithful and just and will forgive us our sins and purify us from all unrighteousness.

ACCEPT – "I accept your free gift of love acceptance and forgiveness and accept you as my personal Lord and Savior from today forward in Jesus name!"

Congratulations. Welcome to the kingdom of God! You are now a Christian – a Christ one!

The good news is that you get to launch into your supernatural life. Paul says it this way in 2 Corinthians 5:17

If anyone is IN Christ you are a new creation, the old has gone, the new has come!

So now you can step into the lifestyle of the supernatural!

You get to practice what you just began!

The good news is we are not alone on this supernatural journey! We have others to help us as well as others who have gone before us.

Hebrews 12:1 says

> *we are surrounded by such a great cloud of witnesses*

The "cloud of witnesses" referred to here are the pioneers who have blazed the way in the supernatural. All of them are cheering us on today!

Your journey into the supernatural has just begun!

CHAPTER 2

Naturally Supernatural

After severely damaging my right knee playing football in my youth, I had a knee replacement operation in 2010 that required me to be hospitalized for a few days. I am a light sleeper, and I soon discovered that hospitals are noisy places. I asked if I could close the door to my hospital room. Up to that time the staff had walked into my room at will and interrupted whatever was happening. But after the door was closed a dramatic change happened which I didn't expect. The staff knocked before they entered and became much more polite towards me.

I realized that simple act had changed the atmosphere in my room. So I began to experiment more. I started playing worship in my room on my iPod. I encouraged and appreciated the staff every time they came in to do something for me.

Their attitudes changed dramatically. So much so that they would spend extra time with me and happily do anything I requested. They even began to open up an talk about themselves and I was able to share God's love with them. Then it culminated on the last day when I was leaving. A nurse escorting me to the front door of the hospital told me all about her life in detail and I was able to share how Jesus had transformed my life and blessed my marriage and children and could do the same for her. This impacted her greatly. What had happened? I had stumbled on a great truth. That you and I can easily change the spiritual atmosphere around us quite easily through a quality decision.

Living in the supernatural is not hard! It is not mystical! It is as natural as you going to sleep at night or getting up in the morning. We just need open our spiritual eyes and see the possibilities.

I was someone who never could sense the supernatural as a young Christian. In fact someone tried to help me understand how simple it was to "see" in the spirit. He told me I was trying too hard! Eventually I realized it was natural for me to be supernatural, and I relaxed. I stopped trying to BE supernatural. I began to learn that during worship or prayer when I felt the presence of the Holy Spirit all I

had to do was to wait and linger there. I started to hear the Holy Spirit whispering things to me that I wouldn't naturally have known. I will share more on how to do this later.

You Were Created For This

The truth is every one of you can live supernaturally. In Genesis 1:26,

> God said, "Let us make mankind in our image, in our likeness..."

God is supernatural! So, if we are created in His image you must created by God to be supernatural too. The bible teaches us that we are made up of three parts. You are a spirit, you have a soul, and you live in a body. Society on the other hand emphasizes just the reverse. It is all about the body. Most things are driven by how you look on the outside of your bodies. Occasionally you are encouraged to take care of your soul. But what about your spirit?

The problem is that most people have never learnt how to live a supernatural life!

It Is Natural for You to Be Supernatural

The supernatural is as natural as you breathing or walking! You don't even think about it. You just do it. Why? Because it naturally happens.

2 Peter 1:3-4 says something very radical. You have everything you need for a supernatural life!

> *His divine power has given us EVERYTHING we need for life and godliness through our knowledge of him who called us by his own glory and goodness. Through these he has given us his very great and precious promises, so that through them YOU MAY PARTICIPATE in the DIVINE NATURE*
>
> ......

So God's divine power has given us the natural ability to

participate in the supernatural. You can have EVERYTHING you need for

> 1) LIFE – Everything you need for a happy fulfilled life
> 2) GODLINESS – Living a supernatural godly lifestyle is possible

Living A Supernatural Life

It is entirely possible for every one of us to walk daily in the supernatural. The good news is that God does not discriminate. It is not just for the especially gifted. You do not have to be Kathryn Kuhlman or Oral Roberts. You can be yourself!

1 Corinthians 14:1 says something very powerful. After the profound teaching on love in the previous chapter, it says

> *eagerly desire gifts of the Spirit*

Another version says "earnestly covet spiritual gifts". To "covet" something normally has a negative connotation. The word "covet" means to "yearn to possess or have something". But here Paul is telling you to passionately desire spiritual gifts. Yes it is good for you to ask God for specific spiritual gifts.

In fact Paul tells us in 1 Corinthians 12:1

> *Now about spiritual gifts, brothers and sisters, I do not want you to be ignorant*

So God does not want us to be ignorant about the different gifts of the Holy Spirit that every believer may have.

When I was a young Christian, I met a man who told me he had just asked God for the gift of faith (see 1 Corinthians 12:7-11). I was staggered. When I questioned him if Christians were allowed to to that he pointed me to this passage in 1 Corinthians 12:1. So I began to desire spiritual gifts too!

The gift that I really wanted and needed as a young pastor was the gift of distinguishing between spirits (also know as the gift of discerning of spirits).

We had a ministry that fed street people and I soon discovered that people would often lie to me trying to get financial assistance. In counselling situations, it was important to discern what was the persons real problem and not just what was presented on the surface. Something unusual began to happen! I began to discern supernaturally when things were wrong in the church and occasionally when people were not telling the truth. This gift began to develop the more it was used.

We went to an international conference each year in Sydney for over a decade. One year a local preacher spoke in an afternoon elective session. I spent the entire time trying to deal with a negative reaction to him in my mind. I thought I had a attitude problem. The following year at that conference the same thing happened when the same preacher got up to speak again. This time I heard the Holy Spirit say, "It is not you who have the problem it is him". A few months later it became public that he has been committing adultery for over 12 months and resigned from being a pastor. The gift of discerning of spirits was working in me and I was learning to be naturally supernatural.

The truth is you already have the Holy Spirit. In fact, Jesus says in Luke 17:21 that the "Kingdom of heaven is within you". So why do Christians spend so much time asking God to fill them over and over again? You need to believe and understand what is already is inside of you!

1 John 2:20 (New King James) says

> *But you have an anointing from the Holy One, and you know ALL things*

Today so many people are hungry to learn about the supernatural. There is so much great teaching now available by teachers like Bill Johnson who have given access to every day people to the supernatural!

My spiritual father Che Ahn teaches that one of the keys to doing ministry today is to follow Jesus' example in John 5:19 when he said

> *I tell you the truth, the Son can do nothing by himself; he can do only what he sees his Father doing, because whatever the Father does the Son also does*

What did Jesus do? He looked with "spiritual eyes" to see what God the father was blessing.

Since we have begun to do this, we have changed the whole way we do ministry. In fact, we are having to unlearn a lot of the church growth teaching and traditional ways of running churches. Why? We are no longer copying techniques or other churches but looking and seeing what the Father is blessing and pouring our resources those things.

One of the most challenging scriptures I read when I first became a Christian was when Jesus said in John 14:12.

I tell you the truth, anyone who has faith in me will do what I have been doing. He will do even greater things than these, because I am going to the Father.

I did not like that bible verse at all! Why was it so challenging? It challenged me beyond my natural understanding. I didn't believe that it was possible for me to "do even greater things" than what Jesus had done here on earth. After all he was the son of God. Obviously, I didn't understand what Jesus had done.

If you want to live supernaturally you must see that Jesus had emptied himself of his Godly attributes and was like any other man including you and I.

Philippians 2:6-8 says Jesus

> *Who, being in very nature God, did not consider equality with God something to be grasped, but made himself nothing, taking the very nature of a servant, being made in human likeness. And being found in appearance as a man..*

He was the same as you and I but he did not sin! Verse 8 continues

> *He humbled himself and became obedient to death — even death on a cross!*

Sadly, even though Jesus prefaced what he said in John 14:12 with

> *I tell you the truth,*

I had deceived myself into thinking it was not possible to live a supernatural life as Jesus did. Like most people who deny the possibility of living a supernatural life, I believed the exact opposite to what Jesus said. I was an UNBELIEVING BELIEVER!

The reality is there is no such thing. Either you believe what Jesus said as a Christ-one or you are not living as a true believer!

Just a few verses later, Jesus reinforces this and explains how you and I can live supernaturally.

First of all, he says in John 14:15

> *If you love me, you will obey what I command.*

What was he speaking about? The need for you to do exactly the same as what He did! Healing the sick, miracles of multiplication, demons obeying you and leaving tormented people, even raising the dead! He did all of this and we will do this and more "IF we love Him and do what He commands"

Then in John 14:16-27 he tells us how you do just that

> *And I will ask the Father, and he will give you another Counsellor to be with you forever— the Spirit of truth. The world cannot accept him, because it neither sees him nor knows him. But you know him, for he lives with you and will be in*

you.

This set me free! I realized it was not up to me to heal anyone or conjure up supernatural signs. The Holy Spirit lives in you and I! It is not you. He will do it through you! You are the conduit for His presence to flow through. You just have to let His power out!

With the Holy Spirit inside you have the same power that raised Christ from the dead living inside of you. Romans 8:11 says just that.

> *And if the Spirit of him who raised Jesus from the dead is living in you, he who raised Christ from the dead will also give life to your mortal bodies through his Spirit, who lives in you.*

He lives inside us. This is the reason why I can say with confidence you can be naturally supernatural!

If we believe God's word is true, then according to 1 Peter 1:4 you will begin to participate in the divine nature. As a result you will experience the supernatural realm more and more naturally each day.

You are even able to take it a step further. You can LIVE IN IT!

There is an old saying that says some people are "so spiritually minded that they are no earthly good". This is an absolute lie. How can I be sure? It contradicts God's word. Just the reverse is true. You can live in the supernatural and natural realm on a daily basis. In fact, this was what you were created to do.

How To Live Supernaturally

How do you live a supernatural life naturally?

Your Conscious Choice

Your freedom to choose is the center of your supernatural experience. It is a divine choice that every human being must make - to live a natural life or a supernatural life. We only become aware of the supernatural growing in us when He opens up our spiritual eyes to 'see'. The New Age calls this your consciousness but there is nothing new under the son! Before the New Age was ever thought of God created every person in His spiritual image. He therefore gave you a conscious choice to live according to the revelation of how you 'see' life. You either 'see' with a natural perspective of life or a supernatural perspective. To move from one to the other requires a choice!

All quality change begins with a realization of truth. The truth is that it is possible to live a "super – natural" life!

All you need to do is decide to begin your supernatural encounter lifestyle!

It is not hard! If I can do it so can you. You just need to give yourself to it. When you do the supernatural will begin to happen in very natural surroundings. You won't have to be in church or praying or even listening to worship in the car. Your spiritual self will start rise up naturally!

In 2002, I was asked by my friend and mentor, Lou Engle,

if I would lead The Call (a National Day of Prayer and Fasting) for our nation of Australia. It would mean two years of planning and mobilization and a huge budget of over $400,000.

After a lot of prayer and seeking counsel from godly friends I accepted. But I didn't know what to do next! Our church was quite small, and I was not a national leader at that time so my influence was small. I decided that God was in it so several of us began to pray.

A few nights later I had very vivid dream. In the dream I went to a national leader of a large denomination and asked his help. In the dream he agreed! The next day

I called for an appointment to see him! But what was I going to say? I felt the Holy Spirit prompt me to tell him about the dream. I took a risk and said to him "I am here because I believe that God told me in a dream to ask you to help me."

He agreed to help instantly and made phone calls immediately to three other national leaders. All four of those leaders became part of the Board of Reference for The Call. On 2nd October 2004, it became a reality when approximately 6000 people stood in the rain in Sydney fasting and praying on behalf of our nation!

It all started with a decision! Why don't you decide right now to live supernaturally from now on?

Recognize What Clutters Your Soul

I have worn glasses since I have turned twenty years

of age. Just recently I was having trouble reading with my glasses and even seeing in a distance. I was very concerned that my eyes were deteriorating and needed to go back to do the optometrists for stronger glasses. When I did go to the optometrist, he didn't even examine my eyes! He just took my glasses and tweaked them and handed them back to me to try. I thought it was miracle! I could see again! What had happened? It seems I had inadvertently sat on my glasses a day or so earlier and they had become out of focus.

The truth is at times your soul gets out of focus too. And it affects your seeing ability. If your soul is cluttered with stuff like worry, stress, offence, unforgiveness and other sin then it will lack peace and self control. This greatly affects your ability to live in the supernatural. Why? Because your spirit is being dominated by your mind, will and emotions.

One of our challenges as Christians is that the world's values have so infiltrated our lives that they have shaped the way we think and love. I attended the National Prayer Breakfast in parliament House in Canberra in 2011. Afterwards, a number of national leaders met to pray and discuss the same sex marriage bill that the Green Party were going to introduce in the Senate later in the year. Up until then it had been difficult to motivate Christians to speak up. Even the non-Christian politicians were asking 'Why are the Christians so quiet'. I believe that the worlds values have so infiltrated our lives the most Christians are numb to the moral changes that are happening around us now!

We need to recognize what clutters our soul and deal

with it.

When Jesus told you and I in John 14:12 that

> *anyone who has faith in me will do what I have been doing.*

The key is to follow what Jesus did!

He then tells you how. He says he will send you another counsellor, He says in verse 18

> *I will not leave you as orphans, I will come to you.*

This is why the father's heart revelation is so important. The orphan spirit affects every person to some degree. In my book "Fathering a Destiny - Growing spiritual sons and daughters" I tell my story.

> **"Even though I have been on a journey of intimacy, the problem for me and most men in western culture is that we have been a part of a fatherless generation. Like so many others, my natural father had problems expressing affection and as a result, like most adult males (and many females) in our culture, had never truly heard my father expressing his love to me. I never had a problem loving Jesus or getting to know the voice of the Holy Spirit within me. But having a deep loving intimate relationship with God my Father seemed far removed because of my experience with my earthly father.**
>
> **Something happened recently to change all that. I**

was at Heidi Baker's Iris Ministries in Mozambique in July 2009. It is Heidi's custom to ask all the visitors to come forward for prayer during her Sunday service. What is unique about this is that she gets the children from their orphanage to lay hands on each visitor and pray for them. My encounter with these children was life changing. They don't pray short, cute prayers for a few minutes. They prayed intense prayers of love and passion for me that lasted thirty minutes. I have never had anyone pray for me that long before let alone two children. After twenty minutes my heart was so moved that I began to weep and weep. I realized that I was the one that was fatherless. I had the orphan spirit while the orphans had been adopted (by Heidi and God the Father). This broke my heart even more. Then something else happened. As they kept praying, I saw a scroll float down from heaven to me. The top of it read 'Certificate of Adoption' and my name was on it! I finally realized that I had been adopted by my Papa Daddy God. I had 'known it' intellectually for over thirty years but this was the first time that it resulted in true intimacy with God. I had a change of identity. I had moved from being an orphan to a son!"

Let me encourage you. If this rings true with you then ask Papa God to help you begin to get free right now! The truth is the only way you can truly live a supernatural life is to grow out of that orphan and get adopted by your heavenly Father!

Why is this so important? An orphan spirit is the main

thing that will clutter our soul.

Romans 8:14 says it best

> Because those who are led by the Spirit of God are sons of God

There is a new emphasis on the Father heart of God in this season of the supernatural. And Papa God is waiting and ready to pour His unconditional love and acceptance into your soul. It's time sons and daughters of God to take your rightful place.

Make Every Effort to Build Your "Spirit"

Years ago we have built a house of prayer in our home. We converted our garage in a wonderful "firehouse" where people come and press into God. Increasingly my wife and I spend time in there just soaking in God's presence. Learning to soak in the Father's love ushers into the realm of the supernatural.

It is possible to build the "supernatural" part of your life. What you feed will grow!

If you feed your supernatural life it will grow! We will deal with this more on a later chapter but for now I want to encourage you to be intentional about only doing the things that feeds your spiritual life!

2 Peter 1:5-7 tells us to make every effort to

> add to your faith goodness; and to goodness, knowledge; and to knowledge, self-control; and to

> *self-control, perseverance; and to perseverance, godliness; and to godliness, brotherly kindness; and to brotherly kindness, love.*

In fact, in 2 Peter 1:8

> *For if we possess these qualities in increasing measure they will keep you from being ineffective and unproductive...*

Verse 10 goes on to say

> *If you do these things you will NEVER FAIL" in living in the realm of the supernatural! Not just for eternity but we can have the supernatural power and presence of God on earth now!*

You can build you spirit. It is not hard. Just choose this is the way you want to live from now on!

Move From Covert To Overt

I began this chapter with my hospital room experience. I inadvertently created a culture within a culture. It was completely different atmosphere outside room.

When I realized the power of what I had done I felt the Holy Spirit was teaching me a lesson! I realized that He wanted me to live like this all the time. I am carrier of the power and presence of the Holy Spirit. So it is possible for me to change the culture or environment wherever I go. And I can do this overtly as a matter of my will. Why? Because Jesus said in Luke 12:32 that as His children

...for it is your Father's good pleasure to give you the kingdom. When we begin to overtly influence our culture this way, we are in fact fulfilling Christ's great commission to all believers to Go and make disciples of all nations In the original Greek translation this was 'pante ethne' - all people groups and cultures!

When you create your own culture, you come from a position of strength. For too long Christians have been seen as weak and dominated under guise that we must be "all things to all men" BUT in reality, all we have done is lost our saltiness and light.

Jesus said in Matthew 5:13

You are the salt of the earth. But if the salt loses its saltiness, how can it be made salty again? It is no longer good for anything, except to be thrown out and trampled by men

It is time you controlled what you let and don't let into your culture

The supernatural was never meant to only for us. Church history tells us that Christians went and hid in cloisters thinking that was the way to experience the supernatural.

We Need to Move to Intentional Influence

Your culture needs to start to influence those from OUTSIDE your culture ON PURPOSE

When you understand that when you are a supernatural

man or woman living a supernatural you naturally take your culture with you.

The more you desire to do this the more it will begin to happen naturally. You will have more divine conversations with people who are hungry for the supernatural but as yet have not met Jesus.

Learn to draw people into our culture by releasing the power of the supernatural in you.

It is entirely possible for you to live this way. Decide you going to live this way from today on.

It is okay! This is how we are meant to live – NATURALLY SUPERNATURAL.

I give you permission to be supernatural.

CHAPTER 3

Choosing To Step Into The Supernatural

My wife Cheryl contacted me from another city where she was attending a national women's conference! She was feeling very oppressed and overcome with intimidation and asked me to pray for her as she did not know what was going on. She did realize what she was experiencing was not a natural reaction but a spiritual encounter. I was so intense that she did not want to be there any longer. After praying for her on the phone I advised her to ask one of our good friends there to personally pray for her. She was reluctant to do that. About two hours later, I was praying for her at home. And I sensed the room shift from a natural realm to a supernatural realm. It was like the wind blowing over a page of an open book. Suddenly I had had glimpse in the spirit realm of exactly what was happening to my wife. I felt the Lord show me that this was her healing and deliverance time. I sensed strongly was in God's perfect will being there. Even better still God was about to set her free from generational fear and intimidation. I told her "You don't need to look for someone to pray for you. God will do it. Press into God. That is what you are good at."

I received the following response late that night "Thank you so much for that word – I believe that you are right and even tonight there was some breakthrough – I am looking for more to come."

What took place? When I moved from the natural realm of reason to the supernatural realm of revelation from the Holy Spirit, my advice changed and it brought breakthrough in the life of another.

The good news is that is both very natural for all of us to experience the supernatural and also very biblical.

You can even choose to live this way on a daily basis! Let me show you how!

In Revelation 1 the Apostle John has a supernatural experience in the midst of his daily life on a fairly normal Sunday. Verse 9 says

> *I, John, your brother and companion in the suffering and kingdom and patient endurance that are ours in Jesus, was on the island of Patmos because of the word of God and the testimony of Jesus. On the Lord's Day I was in the Spirit, and I heard behind me a loud voice like a trumpet.*

Suddenly John has moved from the natural to the supernatural! He heard a voice that sounded like a trumpet. This would be both startling and dramatic.

Instead of being afraid, John wanted to see what was going on. He understood that what he was experiencing felt very normal to him. He didn't have to decide "Now I am going to be spiritual and open my spiritual eyes so I can see in the supernatural." No! He just simply moved from one level to the other without even thinking about it.

So I am not surprised that in Verse 12 we see that he

turned around to see the voice that was speaking to me

The supernatural realm was so real to John that he decided to look at whoever is speaking to him even though he was "in the spirit".

What does "in the spirit" mean? It means that you are

- Able to hear God's voice clearly in the form of ideas that are different to your normal way of thinking. It is always accompanied by His peace
- The atmosphere changes around you so that you sense the presence of God. Sometimes it rushes in other times it gradually increases. Your senses often feel it happening
- An ecstatic consciousness
- Full of the "charisms" or gifts of the Holy Spirit" (see 1 Corinthians 12:7-11, Romans 12:6-8)
- Caught up in a supernatural experience where you are no longer fully aware of your natural circumstances. Instead, you are acutely aware of a supernatural

dimension that you now see. See Saul's conversion in Acts 9:3-4 As he neared Damascus on his journey, suddenly a light from heaven flashed around him. He fell to the ground and heard a voice say to him, Saul, Saul, why do you persecute me?

- Led by spiritual thought instead of natural thinking. Romans 8: 13-14 For if you live according to the sinful nature, you will die; but if by the Spirit you put to death the misdeeds of the body, you will live, because those who are led by the Spirit of God are sons of God.

- Pray in the power of the Holy Spirit where there is a strong sense of God's power and presence on you as you pray. Acts 7:56 Prayer of Stephen "Look," he said, "I see heaven open and the Son of Man standing at the right hand of God."

- Obeying the leading of the Holy Spirit. Acts 8:26 Now an angel of the Lord said to Philip, "Go south to the road—the desert road—that goes down from Jerusalem to Gaza."

- A trance or even being physically taken to another geographical location Acts 8:39 Philip When they came up out of the water, the Spirit of the Lord suddenly took Philip away, and the eunuch did not see him again, but went on his way rejoicing.

All these experiences are biblical and real. All of them involve being caught up in another realm apart from the natural physical realm.

When John turned around, he "saw" more! Even though he was "in the spirit." What he was experiencing involved a supernatural vision, but he also used his natural senses to also comprehend what was happening around him. So, it is possible to use both our natural & supernatural senses at the same time!

Revelation 1:12-16 supports this.

> *I turned around to see the voice that was speaking to me. And when I turned, I saw seven golden lamp stands, and among the lamp stands was someone like a son of man, dressed in a robe reaching down to his feet and with a golden sash around his chest. The hair on his head was white like wool, as white as snow, and his eyes were like blazing fire. His feet were like bronze glowing in a furnace, and his voice was like the sound of rushing waters. In his right hand he held seven stars, and coming out of his mouth was a sharp, double-edged sword. His face was like the sun shining in all its brilliance.*

Now John's response to all of this was not surprising! Verse 17 tells us that when he saw him, he fell at his feet as though dead. But it wasn't because John was overwhelmed by the trance he was having. It was because Jesus the Christ, the king of all kings stood before him in all his glory and majesty. The glorified presence of Jesus was so strong that he could not stand. You and I would respond the same way.

What happens to John next is very important. Verse 17

tells us Jesus placed his right hand on him. John was in a supernatural realm but was still able to experience the physical natural realm at the same time.

Choosing to Step into the Supernatural Realm

It seems that the supernatural is so natural that you can move back and forwards from the natural realm to supernatural realm and back again within the same spectrum of time.

This means that you and I can move freely from the natural realm to the supernatural realm of the kingdom of God at will. This is your true spiritual nature which comes alive when you are become born again! This is what Jesus meant when he said no one can SEE the kingdom of God unless he is born again in John3:3.

When John "sees" the voice of the one speaking behind him in Revelation he is operating out of his regenerated human spirit that came alive when he was born again. So can we!

We become one of the "whoever" of John 3:16. And we enter into the reality of John 3:21

> *whoever lives by the truth comes into the light, so that it may be seen plainly that what they have done has been done in the sight of God.*

John came into the light of the supernatural so he could see when Jesus appeared to him. So can you!

This can be done even more naturally once you open even more to the spirit realm.

Beginnings

For me it began when I first learnt how to "soak" in prayer. I would lie on the floor with a worship on and close my eyes and sing and pray in tongues for a long period of time. After a few of those times I learnt that I had to with all the things from my day and week that was on my mind like you would close a program on a computer. If we don't do this, we are continually having to deal with "soul issues".

A soul issue is any emotion or thought that overtakes and dominates our focus so we cannot concentrate on the thing before us. When you are trying to concentrate on God and His love our mind will often hijack this decision with a subconscious emotion or issue that we have not dealt with. It will come to mind and then you spend your time thinking of that thing instead of worshipping God. This is not evil but the processes of life. When you learn to deal with these things quickly you are then able to press into His presence with ease.

The first time I did this in a church service my mind was opened to the supernatural realm. I "saw" like John even though my eyes were closed. I could see angels in the room. Some were worshipping with us. Others were just standing there with their arms folded waiting. When I asked the Holy Spirit what they were waiting for, He told me they were harvest angels. They were waiting for the gospel to be preached before they would move!

I then opened my eyes and saw the worship leader playing the keyboard. Immediately I "saw" the most beautiful thick long red cloak covering him covered in precious jewels.

I asked God what it was and he told me that was his mantle of anointing.

Now it would have been easy for me to think this was just my imagination. So I thought I would test it to see. When I was introduced as the guest speaker I began by describing what I had seen. Immediately people started shouting praises and praying. I asked the worship leader to come forward. When I began to declare over him that I had seen he began to shake violently and weep. I realized I had truly "seen" for the first time.

But instead of believing that was a once only experience I decided that I would do that every time I would enter worship. I took a risk and did a very bold thing.

During worship at our church I would go and lay down at the front of the church on the carpeted area normally reserved for altar calls. I was ideal thing to do as I found that I was not distracted like normal during worship. Repeatedly the Holy Spirit would give me a word of knowledge or prophetic word for others. They became increasingly clear.

A few months later we were guest speakers at Jubilee church in Sydney. During the worship a lady came forward to give a prophetic word during the worship time. She sang the prophecy instead of speaking it. It was a little off key, and I was initially distracted by that but then I suddenly stepped into the spirit realm. I saw the heart of Jesus surrounded by the hearts of people in the room worshipping His heart. Suddenly Jesus heart expanded and drew all the people's hearts into His heart. When I began to speak, I shared what I saw. Again, the response was dramatic. People began to weep and worship Jesus. God's presence powerfully entered the church very powerfully. When we began to pray for people there was more impact than we had ever seen before.

What was happening? We were learning to experience continually the supernatural in the most natural way.

Choosing to Grow in the Supernatural

Like all natural gifts you possess, the more you hunger for the supernatural and pursue it the more you grow and develop in this realm. When you exercise a natural muscle, it gets stronger. Similarly, if you pursue the Holy Spirit His reality also gets stronger in your life.

You may be tempted to try to analyze what is happening to you but you cannot analyze the Holy Spirit. He moves like the wind. John 3:8 says

> *The wind blows wherever it pleases. You hear its sound, but you cannot tell where it comes from or where it is going. So it is with everyone born of the Spirit.*

According to Jesus in John 14:16 the Holy Spirit is the "spirit of truth".

You do not need to be afraid that you will experience something that is not from God.

The good news is that the Holy Spirit is our teacher.

Jesus said in John 14:26 that

> *The Counselor, the Holy Spirit who the Father will send in name will teach you ALL things...*

This includes the realm of the supernatural.

He is the best teacher you can ever have. He is the real deal. You are not going to get a counterfeit.

1 John 2:27 says it best.

> *As for you, the anointing you received from him remains in you, and you do not need anyone to teach you. But as his anointing teaches you about all things and as that anointing is real, not counterfeit—just as it has taught you, remain in him.*

Some people will never accept this. They just don't get it because they are "carnal" in their thinking. A carnal mind is absorbed by natural desires that are self-destructive. You don't want to live that way. You can't be supernaturally minded if your mind is full of desire! Paul says in Romans 8:6

> *For to be carnally minded is death, but to be spiritually minded is life and peace.* (New King James Version)

A Good Test

The best way to tell if this of God is by its fruit. Here is the way to determine if what you are experiencing is in fact a genuine supernatural experience.

Ask-

- Is there life in your supernatural experiences?

- Does it produce spiritual life and fruit in others when you tell them what you have experienced?
- Do you have more peace? Peace is one of the great testimonies that God is present in someone's life. Peace is the overflow of the supernatural
- Do you love others more? Love is the overflow of a joy filled Jesus centered life

If other people do not understand you don't be concerned.

Kathryn Kuhlman once said

People without the Spirit won't understand. They haven't caught the wonderful Holy Spirit. They simply won't understand how He works or who He is. (1)

Instead choose to continually grow in the supernatural. The Holy Spirit is a great teacher. He will gently coach you into "ever increasing" realms of the spirit.

You will go from being a novice to being one like John who lives "in the spirit".

It is your choice! Why don't you ask the Holy Spirit right now to teach you and to take you deeper into the realm of the His spirit. You will never be the same.

CHAPTER 4

Building An Atmosphere For The Supernatural

One of the keys to understanding how to live in the supernatural is to know how to build the right atmosphere for the supernatural to be present and to increase in your life!

The atmosphere of a room, a home and your life depends on how you live. It is wonderful to enter a room where the people are overflowing with laughter and joy. It is both tangible and very contagious. The reverse is also true. One the most uncomfortable experiences is to enter a room full of tension because of what has been said or done just prior to you entering!

The truth is you create and control the atmosphere around your life! Both in a positive and negative manner. To live a supernatural life, you must decide to create a supernatural culture by how you speak, think and act. This culture is also governed by what you listen to and look out. It is even affected by whom you spend time with.

That is the reason why Paul in his letter to Timothy told him in 1 Timothy 4:7-8 to

> *train yourself to be godly. For physical training is of some value, but godliness has value for all things, holding promise for both the present life and the life to come.*

It is possible to train yourself in the supernatural! Paul goes on to set a (supernatural) example in speech; in life; in in love; in faith; and in purity (verse12). But most importantly Paul says that Timothy (and those who want to grow in the supernatural) should

> *not to neglect the (spiritual) gift which was given to you.*

The Message Bible describes how to do that in verse 16

> *Cultivate these things. Immerse yourselves in them.*

The supernatural life must be cultivated in us. It comes by you immersing yourselves in it! Decide today to create an atmosphere of the supernatural around your life!

It is not just for a select special few! You can do this too. Why don't you choose to do that right now!

Jesus's Example

Jesus understood the importance of creating a supernatural atmosphere. Repeatedly we read in the gospels that after Jesus praying for a person and seeing a miracle all the sick present were then healed. This was because the first miracle resulted in the rest of the people's faith to increase to the point that they could receive too!

The reverse is also true. We are told in Matthew 13:53-58 Jesus had that experience!

> Coming to his hometown, he began teaching the people in their synagogue, and they were amazed. "Where did this man get this wisdom and these miraculous powers?" they asked. "Isn't this the carpenter's son? Isn't his mother's name Mary, and aren't his brothers James, Joseph, Simon and Judas? Aren't all his sisters with us? Where then did this man get all these things?" And they took offense at him.

So even Jesus knew the power of creating an atmosphere for the supernatural. Offense steals from that atmosphere! The reverse is also true. Where there is honor and esteem given to you, it draws the supernatural manifestation out of you to an even greater measure.

People often ask me why we take teams to Africa to practice the supernatural. They reason that we should just do at home in our western nation. The answer is simple! It is easier to learn in atmosphere of the supernatural then in an atmosphere of unbelief.

As well as offence, unbelief limited Jesus moving in the supernatural in his hometown of Nazareth.

Mark 6:5-6 says

> *He could not do any miracles there, except lay his hands on a few sick people and heal them. He was amazed at their lack of faith.*

In the third world nations you can create that atmosphere of faith far more easily!

Why?

Unlike here in the West, they do not have any other alternatives. There is not cheap medicines or free health care like we have in Australia, so they are unable to go to the hospital. They have very little income so they cannot even afford basic antibiotics and medication! Instead, they rely on homemade remedies, witch doctors and the occasional mobile missionary health clinic. But these don't cure their disease! So when you proclaim the power of God through demonstration that Jesus heals then they simply believe. I have seen this with Heidi Baker in Mozambique. After showing the Jesus Movie in their local language and preaching the gospel, Heidi challenges them to bring out their deaf people. After she prays for the first one and they instantly are healed. As a result, everyone believes, and heaven breaks loose. In one night, I personally saw a woman and two children who were completely deaf hear instantly after we prayed for them!

As well in Africa, people are easily healed because they simply believe. Their minds have not been cluttered with so much unbelief from education, skepticism and self-reliance. They have simple faith! And simple faith moves every obstacle no matter how difficult they might be! Jesus said in Matthew 17:20 if we have the faith the size of a mustard seed then mountains would move when we spoke those faith words!

> *I tell you the truth, if you have faith as small as a mustard seed, you can say to this mountain, 'Move from here to there' and it will move. Nothing will be impossible for you.*

Building A Supernatural Atmosphere

To build a supernatural atmosphere you must understand that there are many dimensions to it.

1. Authority

Acts 14:8-10 tells us

> *In Lystra there sat a man who was lame. He had been that way from birth and had never walked. He listened to Paul as he was speaking. Paul looked directly at him, saw that he had faith to be healed and called out, "Stand up on your feet!" At that, the man jumped up and began to walk.*

Paul understood this. The man's healing was NOT dependent on Paul's ability to live or move in the supernatural realm. But he recognized that a key ingredient was present in the other person to be healed. All Paul had to do was to make that COMMAND or DECLARATION of healing and the man was healed.

A friend of mine moves very powerfully in this manifestation of the supernatural. She understands that when you use the authority you have, then things change dramatically in others lives as well as yours. She prayed for a man to be baptized in the Holy Spirit in one meeting in Newcastle. The power of the Holy Spirit hit him so powerfully that the sole of his new pair workbooks was blown right off. What happened? The Holy Spirit came so powerfully that it was like an electricity bolt had hit him. He was healed instantly in the process.

When you speak words of authority, the immovable moves. Your words are so important! God created with His words. As you are created in His image your words create too! They will either build or pull down the spiritual atmosphere around you.

2. Faith Atmosphere

One of the keys to moving in a greater dimension of supernatural power like this is building an atmosphere of faith. Jesus said All things are possible to those who believe. There is substance to faith!

Hebrews 11:1

Now faith is the substance of things hoped for

Faith builds an expectancy. It is contagious.

One of the fathers of the modern healing movement was William Branham. He had a powerful gift of healing. In his meetings in the 1950's, he taught that people had to believe before they would be healed! He continually told people that they had to have faith for their healing. He created an atmosphere of faith using the gift of tongues and testimonies and healing flowed. Though controversial with teachings in his later years, Branham had remarkable signs and wonders happen to him. It started from the day he was born when a supernatural light entered the room just after his birth. As a young boy he heard the audible voice of God calling him to the ministry even though he did not know that it was God's voice at the time. When he would pray for the sick his hand would get cold and swell up if their was a demon present in the person he was praying for. He was most famous for a photo of an angel standing directly behind him when he prayed for people as they filed past him asking for prayer. Amazing healings took place in his meetings. Despite this he would often preach for hours before the healings started to take place. Why? Branham believed that it was the faith atmosphere in the meeting that healed people not him! So that is why he worked so hard to get people to believe! He continually taught people that they had to have faith for their healing. He created an atmosphere of faith when a person testified after they were healed and then healing flowed easily. (1)

Testimonies of people who have been healed will lift the faith of those listening to the point that they also will believe!

You prophesy when you testify! Revelation 19:10 says

testimony of Jesus is the spirit of prophecy

Kathryn Kuhlman used this principle powerfully in her ministry during the 1960's and 70's. Her book "I Believe in Miracles" did not tell her story but consisted of testimonies of miraculous healing. She understood the power of creating an atmosphere of faith to raise the level of expectancy so people would simply believe. (2)

3. The Power Of Tongues

The gift of speaking in other tongues is one of the most unused gifts of the Spirit in the body of Christ today! Many Christians have this gift, but they just don't use it! A lot of Pentecostal Christians today are Pentecostal by heritage only! Maybe they had an spiritual experience once but do not actively pursue the use the gifts of the Holy Spirit daily.

But there is a new day here now! There is a growing hunger for experiencing the supernatural today!

The good news is that it is easy to cultivate a supernatural atmosphere in your life. One of the best ways is to speak in tongues. You can easily do this while worship is being played in your home or as you are driving in your car.

Tongues moves you out of the natural into the supernatural.

In 1 Corinthians 14:4, Paul says

He who speaks in a tongue edifies himself...

The Amplified Bible says that you edify and improve yourself. In other words, it builds your supernatural being!

For many people today who have received the baptism of the Holy Spirit, they treat the gift of tongues as an optional extra or even a strange oddity. Yet the gift of tongues opens up the realm of the supernatural.

In Romans 8:26-27 Paul says

> *In the same way, the Spirit helps us in our weakness. We do not know what we ought to pray for, but the Spirit himself intercedes for us through wordless groans. And he who searches our hearts knows the mind of the Spirit, because the Spirit intercedes for God's people in accordance with the will of God.*

The Message says it this way

> *Meanwhile, the moment we get tired in the waiting, God's Spirit is right alongside helping us along. If we don't know how or what to pray, it doesn't matter. He does our praying in and for us.*

I have personal experience of how powerful tongues are for creating an atmosphere for the supernatural. When I was in Korea in 2010 to teach at a Wagner Leadership Institute in Jangyu province, I experienced an unusual phenomenon. The class would always worship for a long time before I was introduced to speak. Even though I knew the songs very well I had trouble singing the English words when my friends were all singing in Korean. All of a sudden even the verses of simple songs like "How great is our God" were forgotten by me. After a while I decided to sing in tongues instead. After twenty minutes of just singing in tongues something remarkable happened. The realm of the supernatural opened. I started to see angels in the room. When I did open my eyes God gave me words of knowledge and prophecies for every person I looked at. Later I was able to release those words over each of them as I prayed for them one after another.

From that time on, at the beginning every class, the same thing happened! What had taken place? I had learned to build a supernatural atmosphere that I could freely enter and hear God very clearly!

Pray in the gift of tongues, it will help build the supernatural realm around you.

You can learn to create your own supernatural atmosphere too! Why don't you begin now?

CHAPTER 5

A Generation Of The Double Encounter

Wisdom says you need to understand the 'times' you live in. When you look back over the past fifty years you significant changes in society. There has been an acceleration in technology, education and humanism. There has also been an acceleration in the decline of values and an erosion of the foundations of society such as biblical marriage and family. In the midst of this is a generation that is not satisfied. Those in this generation are hungry for more! Who is this generation? You are! If you are reading this book with a hungry heart than you are this generation!

This is the generation of supernatural. There is more hunger for spiritual realm and living in the power of the Holy Spirit than there has been since the charismatic renewal of the traditional church in the 1970's.

Do you realize how significant time we are in?

Right now, there are more hotspots of revival and signs

of awakening in the western world than before. There is an "acceleration" in the supernatural process that has ALREADY come into the body of Christ.

Isaiah 60:1 declares prophetically to you today

> *Arise, shine, for your light has come, and the glory of the LORD rises upon you.*

The light of revival has already come! We need to stop saying "revival is coming". It is already here!

We have to recognize it and then step into it.

This Is The Season Of Double Supernatural Encounters

This acceleration in believers experiencing the supernatural realm is exciting. It truly is a season of double encounters for those who are willing!

What used to take us months and years before is now being received and activated by us now in an instant.

There are many examples of this in revival history. One of best is the manifestation of the baptism of the Holy Spirit. After Pentecost and the rise of the early church, there are only isolated incidents in church history of the manifestation of the baptism of the Holy Spirit.

Then in 1906 at Azusa Street in Los Angeles, Pastor William Seymour began to preach and wait for the manifestation of the spirit. They were "tarrying meetings" where people would tarry or wait for days and even weeks for the power of the Holy Spirit to fall.

However, when the charismatic renewal took place in the 1970's people did not need to tarry. Instead, they received the baptism in an instant! What happened? They it received by faith and instantly stepped into it! What did they do? They asked the Father for the promised gift of the Holy Spirit. Then they received it by faith and began to speak in tongues and then the wind of the spirit came'

Bill Johnson's teaching today on the Kingdom of God has met a hunger of believers in the body of Christ. We are beginning to understand that it is God's will for every Christian to heal the sick and to experience the supernatural as the normal part of daily Christian living.

In Luke 9:1 we are told Jesus

> *gave them power and authority to drive out all demons and to cure diseases*

Then in Luke 10:1 Jesus gave the disciples (that means you too if you are a born again believer in Jesus Christ) authority to heal the sick and cast demons out of people. This is Christianity 101! Every Christian has the power & the authority to do just that!

If this is true, then this means this is your season where you will encounter the demonstration of Spirit's power by ALL believers.

The truth is that there has been enough talk and not enough demonstration. 1 Corinthians 4:20 says it this way

> *But the Kingdom of God is not a matter of talk*

but of power.

You can do this!

Jesus tells us Luke 17:21 that

> *...the kingdom of God is within you.*

Let out what's inside you. It is not your responsibility to heal the sick! That is not your job. That is God's job!

Our role is to be ministers of the Holy Spirit. 2 Corinthians 3:6 tells us

> *He has made us competent as ministers of a new covenant—not of the letter but of the Spirit; for the letter kills, but the Spirit gives life.*

If you are ministers of the spirit, then you need to minister the Holy Spirit to people you pray for. Most Christians don't have a clue how to do this. Often when I see people praying for others, they don't not minister the Holy Spirit. Instead, they appear to be giving people a back massage as they pray! That is not what it means to lay hands on someone!

Instead realize that you have the same spirit that raised Christ from the dead is living in you (Romans 8:11). Therefore, your job is to only release what is inside of you to others.

This Season Of Acceleration Is Also The Anointing Of Double

The question is how does that work?

A GENERATION OF THE DOUBLE ENCOUNTER

How do you step into the anointing of double?

In Judges 1 we see a change of God's generals. Verse 1 says Joshua died. When generals die, it signifies that God is about to release a whole new season of leadership and whole new anointing.

In January 2009, a mentor of mine, Jill Austin died unexpectedly. She was one of the generals of the Jesus people movement in the late 1960's and 1970's and a prophet who taught the body of Christ how to how to prophetically flow in the presence and power of the Holy Spirit. Jills's death was prophetic.

It signified one era of the kingdom of God had finished and another had begun.

On December 15, 2009, Oral Roberts, a father in the faith and pioneer of the healing evangelism movement from the late 1940's forward, went home to be with the Lord. His teaching on how to expect miracle became one of the pillars for most of the teaching on the supernatural today. A general passed into glory.

Then on March 26, 2010, Freda Lindsay, a general who founded 'Christ For The Nations' ministry training institute alongside her late husband Gordon, died.

'Christ For The Nations' global reach extends to 120 nations, and 11,000 churches. Gordon Lindsay was the manager for William Branham in the early days of the healing revival in the 1950's. But Freda and Gordon Lindsay are most famous for Voice of Healing magazine which fanned into flame the beginning of the modern-day healing ministry that so many have followed since. Another general had gone to glory.

Three generals died in a short space of time!

It is important that you always take note when generals die in the body of Christ because God is about to release a new level of authority and power and especially a new level of glory.

Typically, a change like this is accompanied by a shift or a new wind of Spirit, manifestations of new level of glory.

In Judges 1:8-14 tells us Judah attacked Jerusalem also and took it.

> *They put the city to the sword and set it on fire. After that, Judah went down to fight against the Canaanites living in the hill country, the Negev and the western foothills. They advanced against the Canaanites living in Hebron and defeated Sheshai, Ahiman and Talmai. From there they advanced against the people living in Debir. And Caleb said, "I will give my daughter Aksah in marriage to the man who attacks and captures Kiriath Sepher." Othniel son of Kenaz, Caleb's younger brother, took it; so Caleb gave his daughter Aksah to him in marriage. One day when she came to Othniel, she urged him to ask her father for a field. When she got off her donkey, Caleb asked her, "What can I do for you?"*

Now this story is told twice in bible (see also Joshua 15:9).

This signifies importance.

Caleb asked his daughter Acsah "What can I do for you?" It seems that Father God is also asking His sons and daughters the same question today!

Today Father God Is Asking What Can He Do For You

Our Father Papa God is asking you right now "What can he do for you?".

It is a very important question. He is not asking about what possessions you want or your kingdom of self (not your future, your relationships, your kingdom) but His Kingdom in you!

It is all about your thirst for God's glory.

How thirsty are you for the supernatural manifestation of God through you?

As a child, I was in the Boys Scouts for many years. They taught me many invaluable life skills including how to survive in the bush even without food or water. I know what it is to walk for miles after we have run out of water. The thirst is hard to describe. But when you drink for the first time. It overcomes you with the feeling of refreshing and life! This is the season we are in.

In Joshua 1:15 Caleb's daughter says to her father

Do me a special favor.

You need to know that Papa God delights to do favours for his children. Jesus teaches us this in Luke 12:32

> *Do not fear, little flock, for it is your Father's good pleasure to give you the kingdom. (NKJV)*

He loves to bless His children with the kingdom of heaven. What part of His kingdom do you want to have in life today?

I have a good friend who often tells me that they are God's favorite. They are right. They are God's favorite and so are you! Believe it and begin to declare it! You will begin to experience God's favor too the more you grow in intimacy with father God. He delights in blessing his sons and daughters.

Kevin Dedmon in his great book 'The Ultimate Treasure Hunt" (2) teaches us that when Jesus heard God's audible voice at his water baptism in Luke 3:22

> *You are my son, whom I love; with you I am well pleased.*

something great took place inside of Him. When you hear your Father God say "YOU ARE MY SON / MY DAUGHTER. I LOVE YOU AND I AM PLEASED WITH YOU" then His heart is released into you. You know you are His favorite from then on!

You Need A Father's Heart Revelation

Today you need a fresh father's heart revelation. He loves you! So much so He is IN LOVE with you! He delights in giving you, His kingdom.

This is why His favor is on you. His heart's desire is to

bless you with more of His presence.

I spent 33 years of being a Christian without this revelation. Three years ago I finally stepped into it. Today ask Father God to adopt you with His Father's heart. You will never be alone again. You will no longer be an orphan with a orphan spirit. You will experience a whole new way of living and loving as God's favorite.

What favor does Acsah ask her daddy Caleb for?

Judges 1:15 tells us

> She replied, "Do me a special favor. Since you have given me land in the Negev, give me also springs of water.

Jesus spoke a a lot about springs of water. In John 4 he had an encounter with the woman from Samaria. He told her about how she could drink "living water" (verse 10) and all she had to do was to ask him for it.

Then in John 7:38, Jesus declared to all present at the Feast of Tabernacles

> *If anyone thirsts, let him come to Me and drink.*
> *He who believes in Me, as the Scripture has said,*
> *out of his heart will flow rivers of living water.*

Not a trickle or intermittent flood after years of drought, but an ongoing river of living water flowing through you.

So often a Christian's life ranges between a flood or a drought. They can go from the heights of a supernatural conference to the depths of not even sensing God is with them.

But God the Father wants you to have a constant life-giving revival spring inside you!

How Do You Get The River Flowing?

This is a great question. Declare you have living water inside of you. It is time to unplug the flow. It is time to get your river flowing. Numbers 21:17 says it best

Spring up, O well!...

Shout about it!

Speak to the spring inside of you right now.

Command it to spring up! Spring up!

River flow in Jesus' name!

You can have this river that just keeps springing up over and over and over again. You have the overflow of Holy Spirit revival anointing and it is here now for you because you are His favorite!

But wait there is more!

What happens next to Caleb's daughter Acsah will surprise you.

The Generation of The Double

Even though she had already received her inheritance of land when Acsah asked her father Caleb for an extra inheritance, she asked boldly for the best - the springs of water!

Most Christians today are satisfied to have received their salvation inheritance. Eternal life is awesome. But there is more if you are prepared to ask your heavenly Father for it! You can have springs of water rising up inside of you too!

What amazes me is that God loves not only to give us what we have asked for, but He also wants to give us double!

Acsah didn't realize what she was about to receive. She received double what she had asked her father for!

Judges 1:15 tells us what happened.

Then Caleb gave her the upper and lower springs.

You are a part of the 'Generation of the Double.' Right here, right now! Not just for young ones or only those who you think are more qualified, but for ALL the Sons of God. And that means you too!

We are in a season of acceleration where we will receive a double portion overflow. Where others had to fight to receive, tarry and intercede for decades, you can have it right here, right now!

You Only Have To Ask The Father For It

Like Caleb's daughter you only have to ask your Father for it.

We need the same attitude. Expect the double manifestation of His glory.

You can boldly ask for it!

Now some may argue that this is presumptuous. No, Jesus said just the reverse. Jesus said it. It is the Father's good pleasure to give you HIS kingdom. (Luke 12:32)

Notice I didn't say your kingdom! It's not about you - your wants or desires! But HIs kingdom on earth being displayed here on earth through you!

It is okay! He has given you permission to ask for it.

You Will Receive Even More

It pleases the Father when you ask him for more!

This is so contrary to what has been taught over the past two hundred years in Christian circles. For too long there has been a false humility mentality that it is proud to ask for more. But Jesus himself said in Matthew 7:7

> ASK and it WILL BE given to you; seek and you will find; knock and the door will be opened to you.

We quote the "seek and you will find" part but not the "ask" part. It is time to do what Jesus said! Ask for more of Him!

But Jesus wasn't finished! He then said in Matthew 7:8

> For EVERYONE who asks receives; he who seeks finds; and to him who knocks, the door will be opened.

God will do the same for you as He does for me!

ASK ASK ASK!!!

And then get ready to receive!

What is surprising is that you will receive even more than

you ask for.

In Judges 1, Acsah asked for 'springs of water' – her father gave her double what she asked for! He gave her the upper and lower rivers. She got double of what she asked for. And so will you as this is the heart of the Father for you too!

When I was a young leader, I met Clark Taylor. He came to our church in 1986 to open our new church building as a favor to my senior leader. It was my responsibility to be his driver. As we drove from the hotel, he began to teach me how the Holy Spirit loved us learning about the supernatural. He told me that the more we ask the more the Holy Spirit teaches us and gives us new insights into the spirit realm. He declared that you can even practice using what He has given to you. Not only does the Holy Spirit enjoy us doing that but also He wants us to ask for more and more of His presence!

As Jesus said in Mark 11:24

> *Therefore, I tell you, whatever you ASK for in prayer, BELIEVE that you have received it, and it WILL be yours*

Expect to receive what Apostle Paul called ever increasing glory.

He tells us in 2 Corinthians 3:18

> *And we all, who with unveiled faces contemplate the Lord's glory, are being transformed into his image with ever-increasing glory, which comes from the Lord, who is the Spirit.*

What else does that mean?

It is time for you to go from one level of glory to the next level.

Its next level revival time and its double.

Today God is saying to you "What can I do for you?"

Ask right now for springs of water.

Be a part of the Double Generation!

Receive DOUBLE revival and DOUBLE springs of glory!

CHAPTER 6

The Power Of The Holy Spirit's Overflow

Dominating The Kingdom of Darkness

We were ministering in a church a while ago and there was a constant theme throughout the testimonies, the prayer requests and the church notices. Over and over, we heard how powerful the Satan's attacks were against members of that church. The more I asked questions and listened to their responses it became obvious to me that there wasn't any specific spiritual warfare going on! It was a wrong mindset that they had adopted! They believed that the Christian life was a never-ending struggle against the power of the enemy.

Ephesians 6:12 does say that we struggle against the powers of this dark world. I do not underestimate the enemy! All good armies need to be aware of the strategies of how their enemy attacks! But I have discovered that you can also live confidently and victoriously through the posture of faith and the position of victory.

Your wrestle is a rest!

A rest of faith!

I don't have any concern about the enemies' plans!

And if you are a believer, you should not too!

Instead, I have got good news! We have already won the victory through the shed blood of Jesus the Christ.

As Revelation 12:11 says

> *They (blood washed believers IN Christ) overcame (this is in the past tense as Jesus said IT IS FINISHED) him (the devil) by the blood of the Lamb (Jesus THE Christ) and the word of their testimony.*

In other words, Jesus has already conquered sin, hell and death through shedding His blood for us. We just need to enter that victory by faith.

Know Your Authority

The only challenge is we must get our position and testimony right!

Our position is that satan is under our feet. This is how we will never give the devil a foothold. Paul says in Ephesians 4:27 not to do that!

Our position only becomes clear to us when we realize exactly who is inside us! Jesus said in Luke 17:21

The kingdom of heaven is within you.

He told us in John 7:38 that

> Whoever believes in me, as the scriptures have said, streams of living water will flow from him.

It is so important that we realize WHO is inside us!

In addition to believing in Jesus as your Savior, you must believe that Jesus is lives inside you!

Romans 8:11 sums it up the best.

> And if the spirit of him who raised Christ from the dead will also give life to your mortal bodies through his Spirit who lives in you.

Several years ago, I heard a very sad story of a homeless man in Chicago who was sleeping in his car during winter. He would regularly start the engine during the night so the heater would keep him from becoming too cold.

However eventually he ran out of fuel in the car and on one extremely cold night he froze to death! The story gets sadder when the police notified his next of kin.

They discovered that attorneys had been looking for the man to notify him that three months before he had inherited millions of dollars from a distant relative. He never knew what his inheritance was. He did not have to live that way at all!

When I heard that story in the media, I heard the Holy Spirit whisper to me

This is how most of my sons and daughters live. They

do not know their true inheritance.

You will spend your entire life trying to fight external forces with your own strength if you do not realize who is inside you.

The truth is that Jesus has already taken dominion over all darkness in this world! You and I are no longer under his dominion! We are under the dominion of another - the King of Kings and the Lord of Lords!

The answer is to start believing and acting like you have dominion over darkness too!

Now for some time a man named Simon had practiced sorcery in the city and amazed all the people of Samaria."

This is best illustrated in the book of Acts.

Acts 8:5 tells us that Philip went down to the city of Samaria and proclaimed Christ there. What happens next can only be described as a clash of two spiritual kingdoms.

Phillip went to Samaria when Paul started to persecute all the believers in Jerusalem. He proclaimed the Gospel of Jesus Christ there.

Acts 8:6 says that the miraculous signs compelled the people to listen carefully to what he had to say.

This is a chief purpose of a sign and wonder. The people see a miraculous sign from God and it causes them to wonder about their need for Christ's salvation for them and the lack of God's help, love, life in their life.

Simon, the sorcerer was also there, and he also had

supernatural power – in fact, people called him the 'Great Power'.

But it was not God's power.

Christians sometimes see the power of the enemy and get intimidated!

But I believe that we must have the same attitude as Smith Wigglesworth who woke one night to find satan standing at the bottom of his bed. Smith dismissively said

"Hmm! It is only you" and turned over and went back to sleep.

You need to know that Jesus in you is greater than any other spiritual force.

God tells us just that in I John 4:4

> *You, dear children, are from God and have overcome them, because the one who is in you is greater than the one who is in the world*

In my book, "Fathering a Destiny - Growing Spiritual Sons and Daughters" I share a story about talking our golden cocker spaniel dog for a walk!

We were ambushed by a very large dog that was aggressively advancing from behind us ready to attack.

I turned and said one word with great authority

"No!"

The dog stopped in its tracks and turned on its heals and ran away.

The Holy Spirit taught me a lesson that day that I have never forgotten!

That is the way you speak to the devil - like you would address a naughty dog that you have authority over.

In Acts 8, we are told the story of Simon the Sorcerer who had some influence in Samaria because of his magical powers.

But it was no match for the power of God.

When Simon encountered Phillip, Acts 8:12 tells us that Simon was ASTONISHED by the great signs and miracles that he saw.

Why?

Because Jesus power was and will always be so much greater than anything that satan can do!

Satan has been defeated once and for all. We just need to believe it!

The result was that Simon believed the good news of Jesus Christ and declared through his baptism to all who had been following him that he was now a follower of Jesus.

What happened?

The kingdom of heaven overtook and dominated the kingdom of darkness.

Actually, it was no contest. It was a one-way victory. As Revelation 11:5 says

> "The kingdoms of this world have become the kingdom of our Lord and of his Christ, and he will

reign for ever and ever".

Every believer needs to enter into that victory today! You can do it right now! Choose to no longer be under the influence of delusion of the kingdom of darkness. Instead choose to rise up up into your true position and authority as one who dominates the kingdom of darkness.

Know Who You Are

You need to know who you are in Christ. You do not have to raise you voice. The demons must obey you. You already have authority! I call it Christianity 101! Jesus the Christ has given you the same authority to us over demons and sickness that he gave to his disciples.

In Luke 9:1 Jesus had called the Twelve together and

He gave them power and authority to drive out all demons and to cure diseases.

You must believe that you already have that authority. Believe what is already is in you.

Luke 10:18-19 tells us that satan has already fallen from heaven.

As a born-again believer, he is already under your feet.

Nothing will hurt you. You have nothing to fear.

Jesus said this in Luke 10:19

I have given you authority to trample on snakes and scorpions and to overcome all the power of the enemy; nothing will harm you.

You are not using your authority but the authority of Jesus the Christ! Know who you are and know the authority that in you.

Know Your Peace

If you find that when you experience unexpected trials and attacks you lose the presence of peace (or your awareness of the supernatural realm) than you have not spent enough time in God's presence each day. The level of your peace when things go wrong is your supernatural presence gauge!

If you do not soak in the supernatural presence of God, enough each day the pressures of life and the attacks of the enemy will cause you to step out of your peace realm and into your emotions. Instead of peace you will live in stress, worry frustration or even fear! Once there you are susceptible to the realm of oppression and defeat.

What do you when you find yourself or someone else continually oppressed by negative emotions or circumstances? The Apostle Peter taught in Acts 3 that

> *times of refreshing comes from the presence of the Lord.*

To experience this freedom, you have to dramatically change the direction of your thought process. Peter said the way to do this is to "repent."

This is a word that has a negative reputation but in reality it is way to life. When genuinely humble yourself before Jesus Christ and turn as act of your will from your old ways of thinking and acting, then break through and freedom comes. Peter put it this way in Acts 3:19

> *Repent, then, and turn to God, so that your sins may be wiped out, that times of refreshing may come from the Lord*

This is what the Bible calls "deliverance."

Deliverance removes all the barriers for you to encounter God's love and then live in the supernatural peace of Jesus Christ!

Prayer Of Deliverance

This is what you decide to do when you or someone else has oppression or demonic activity harassing their lives and do not have peace. First the person if they want to be free. If they do, you may choose to use this suggested prayer based on the teachings of Derek Prince "They Shall Expel Demons". They will be set free!

Pray This Prayer Of Deliverance: -

Lord Jesus Christ, I believe you are the son of God and the only way to God . I believe that you died on the cross for all of my sins and overcame death and the power of evil through your resurrection so that I might be forgiven and receive eternal life.

I renounce all pride and self-importance. I believe that you died in my place to set me free.

I confess all my sins before you and especially the sins of ....

I repent of all sins. I turn away from them and I turn completely to you, and accept your free gift of love and forgiveness"

I renounce all false religions and all involvement I have had in the occult in particular ....

I forgive everyone who has hurt me especially (name them) .... and let go of all hurt, offence, unforgiveness and bitterness.

I thank you that on the cross you took every curse for me so that I could be free from every curse over my life.

I stand with you, Lord, against all Satan's demons. I submit to you Lord Jesus Christ and resist the devil.

Amen

Divine Healing

For some reason the subject of healing causes more controversy in the media than any other subject of the supernatural. But I have not found a person who want to remain ill! Health is better than sickness!

Why are people so afraid?

It is the fear of the supernatural rather than any false hope argument that critics may use.

The opposition to divine healing is very similar to the opposition in the origins of the practice of medicine. In the

Middle Ages most practitioners were accused of alchemy. But getting better is then staying sick!

So, you have nothing to lose and everything to gain! So why not open your thinking to the supernatural realm of divine healing!

Divine healing occurs when a person who is ill or has a permanent disability is healed without a natural reason or medical intervention.

When you read the Gospels in the New Testament you will see that Jesus spent more time healing the sick and casting out evil spirits including the spirit of infirmity than any other thing.

Why? The Holy Spirit inside Him was more powerful than other natural condition of the person.

As we have seen in Luke 9:1 Jesus has also given his disciples that same power and authority to drive out all demons and to cure diseases.

Then in Luke 9:2 he also

sent them out to preach the kingdom of God and to heal the sick

The good news that Jesus not only has taken our sins but also our sickness. It was prophesied five hundred years before as recorded by the prophet Isaiah. He declared that Jesus, would come and take our infirmities as well as our sin.

In Isaiah 53:4-5

Surely he took up our infirmities and carried our

> *sorrows, yet we considered him stricken by God, smitten by him, and afflicted.*
> *But he was pierced for our transgressions, he was crushed for our iniquities; he punishment that brought us peace was upon him, and by his wounds we are healed*

Then when Peter quoted the same part of the prophecy after the death and resurrection of Christ he changed the tense of the verse to the past tense in 1 Peter 2:24 to

> *………. by his wounds you have been healed*

Why the change?

Because it was finished!

Christ had become both Savior and Healer for you and I!

So healing is part of Christ's work salvation for us! It is what He has done for all of us. So, you never have to pray again "IF it is your will Lord?" It is ALWAYS His will to heal you!

We need to believe that God gives life and health. Jesus does not give sickness or death but only life. Jesus said himself in John 10:10

> *The thief comes only to steal and kill and destroy; I have come that they may have life, and have it to the full.*

All you have to do is to believe! And do as Jesus said in Mark 16:17-18

And these signs will accompany those who believe: In my name they will drive out demons; they will place their hands on sick people, and they will get well.

You get what you believe for! All you need to do is to believe! It is not your job to heal the sick. That is what the Holy Spirit does. But we are the ministers of that healing power!

James puts it this way in James 5:14-15

Is any one of you sick? He should call the elders of the church to pray over him and anoint him with oil in the name of the Lord. And the prayer offered in faith will make the sick person well; the Lord will raise him up.

Who heals? The Lord does!

Your job is to the prayer of faith and to minister that healing presence or anointing that you have inside of you.

Many people ask how to pray for divine healing. So here is a simple way to pray for healing.

How To Pray For Healing

ASK THE HOLY SPIRIT - Ask the Holy Spirt to reveal the root cause of the sickness. Just don't listen to what the person says is wrong with them.

Pray. The Holy Spirit will give the answer. AND ASK THE HOLY SPIRIT HOW YOU PRAY FOR THEM. Listen to what He says to you and do it!

RENOUNCE SICKNESS - If sickness is not from God, then it can be renounced! James 4:7

> *"Resist the devil and he will flee from you."*

Get the person to refuse to allow the infirmity to stay in their body any longer!

CONFESS AND ASK FORGIVENESS FOR ALL SINS - 1 John 1:9 - And ask the person to surrender their life to the will of God.

JESUS IS YOUR HEALER - Matthew 8:17

> *"He took our infirmities and carried our diseases".*

1 Peter 2:24

> *"He himself bore our sins" in his body on the cross, so that we might die to sins and live for righteousness; "by his wounds you have been healed."*

Ask them to declare "Jesus thank you that you are my healer. I RECEIVE CHRIST AS MY SAVIOUR FROM SICKNESS AS WELL AS MY SINS. Believe

that Jesus took their sickness as well as their sins on the cross in their place. Psalms 103:3, Isaiah 53:5, Luke 13:16

RECEIVE THEIR HEALING BY FAITH - Mark 1:25

> *"Therefore I tell you, whatever you ask for in prayer, believe that you have received it, and it will be yours."*

YOU ARE THE MINISTER OF THE NEW COVENANT HERE ON EARTH (which includes healing and health) so NOW lay hands on them and impart the Holy Spirit's healing presence into them in Jesus name - 2 Corinthians 3:6, Mark 16:17-18

EXPECT THE POWER OF THE HOLY SPIRIT TO FLOW THROUGH YOU AS YOU MINISTER HEALING AND HEALTH - Mark 16:17-18

See Appendix 1 - For a larger list of healing references in the Bible of God healing us and us praying for the healing of others

The Overflowing Power Of The Holy Spirit

I always wanted everything God had to give me. So should you! The main reason you need the baptism of the Holy Spirit is is that you need His power to live and move in the supernatural!

The last thing Jesus said to ALL the believers before he ascended into heaven is in Acts 1:8

> But you will receive power when the Holy Spirit comes on you; and you will be my witnesses in Jerusalem, and to the ends of the earth.

It is also referred to by Jesus as the promise of the Father and the baptism of the Holy Spirit by John the Baptist and the apostles in the early church in the book of Acts. But the terminology is not important. What is important is the fact that it is a doorway into a greater realm of the supernatural.

It is all about having His power to be the most effective spiritual life that you can! To live a supernatural life, you need supernatural power!

In Luke 3:16 it is John who declares that Jesus is the one who baptizes with the Holy Spirit and with fire!

> *I baptize you with water. But one more powerful than I will come, the thongs of whose sandals I am not worthy to untie. He will baptize you with the Holy Spirit and with fire.*

When His fire comes into you then you change! You are empowered with boldness!

Even the quietest most timid person can become full to overflowing. When that the baptism - river of life is turned on inside of you and boldness and authority will flow out of you!

One of my daughters is a great example of this. She has a very quiet and gentle nature. But since he has been baptized in the Holy Spirit she overflows with boldness. In public places she boldly asks complete strangers who are obviously sick is she can pray for divine healing for them. They say yes and she prays and sees dramatic changes in their level of heath. How can she be so bold? She has learnt to allow the Holy Spirit to overflow through her life. And you can too!

The Holy Spirit is your helper and your teacher. Jesus said in John 14:16-17 that He becomes your Counsellor as the "Spirit of truth".

In John16:13 Jesus also says

> *But when he, the Spirit of truth, comes, he will guide you into all truth. He will not speak on his own; he will speak only what he hears, and he will tell you what is yet to come.*

So, you have nothing to fear. Your life will continue to get better as you learn to listen to His truth.

In the Book of Acts from Acts 2 onwards you can read what the baptism of the Holy Spirit did to ordinary people. It doesn't matter how qualified or spiritual you may feel, your life will dramatically change once you receive the baptism of the Holy Spirit.

Remember that it is a gift that you must receive and then use. Here are some simple steps that will help receive the empowering of the Holy Spirit that will only the door even wider for you into the supernatural!

How To Receive The Overflowing Power (Baptism) Of The Holy Spirit

ASK - Have you asked Jesus Christ to be your Savior and Lord of your life? If not ask Him right now! ASK Him to take control and ACCEPT His free gift of love acceptance and forgiveness

PRAY - Pray for any known or unknown sin. Take a moment and do that right now. Ask Jesus to forgive you and cleanse you.

Romans 10:8-10

> *"But what does it say? "The word is near you; it*

> is in your mouth and in your heart," that is, the
> message concerning faith that we proclaim: If
> you declare with your mouth, "Jesus is Lord," and
> believe in your heart that God raised him from
> the dead, you will be saved. For it is with your
> heart that you believe and are justified, and it is
> with your mouth that you profess your faith and
> are saved."

ENQUIRE - Have you had any involvement in the occult? Including horoscopes, fortune telling and any new age teaching?

If so, you need confess each one as sin and renounce their control over your life. Read Deuteronomy 18:10-13

DECLARE FREEDOM - I John 1:9

> "If we confess our sins, he is faithful and just and
> will forgive us our sins and purify us from all
> unrighteousness."

Declare - " I am forgiven and cleansed according to God's word"

FAITH - "Have you faith to receive the baptism in the Holy Spirit?" THEN ASK AND RECEIVE - LUKE 11:9-10

> "Ask and it will be given to you; seek and you will
> find; knock and the door will be opened to you.
> For everyone who asks receives"

Ask the Father to baptise you right now!

UNDERSTAND - God will give you a personal prayer

language that comes with the baptism.

It releases power into a believer's life. READ ACTS 2:4, ACTS 10:45-16 & 1 CORINTHIANS 14:4-5.

There is a difference between the gift of tongues in a church worship setting & personal prayer language.

See ROMANS 8:26. THE MAIN NEED FOR THE BAPTISM - POWER TO BE

BOLD BELIEVER - ACTS 1:8 "You shall receive power when the Holy Spirit

BE CONFIDENT THAT YOU WILL RECEIVE THE HOLY SPIRIT - LUKE 11:11-13

> *"Which of you fathers, if your son asks for a fish, will give him a snake instead? Or if he asks for an egg, will give him a scorpion? If you then, though you are evil, know how to give good gifts to your children, how much more will your Father in heaven give the Holy Spirit to those who ask him!"*

YOU NEED TO BELIEVE THAT YOU WILL RECEIVE THE BAPTISM OF THE HOLY SPIRIT WHEN YOU ASK FOR IT!

PRAY - Pray this prayer. "Father God, I ask that you baptize me in the Holy Spirit. I receive it by faith in Jesus name. I will praise you now in a new prayer language. Amen"

BEGIN TO PRAY OUT LOUD - BEGIN TO SPEAK OUT THE WORDS THAT BEGIN TO OVERFLOW AS YOU PRAISE GOD OUT LOUD - Not in English but whatever that comes to your lips. Keep going! Don't stop!

IF YOU DID NOT SEE AN OUTWARD OVERFLOW. This is a gift is there to be unwrapped, and you need to expect their language to come sometime when you are praising the Lord!

USE THE POWER - The key to growing in the overflowing power of the Holy Spirit is to USE the baptism every day. THE KINGDOM OF GOD IS INSIDE YOU

- Luke 17:21.

Let it out by praying for the sick, praying in your prayer language, asking God for divine encounters to increase your understanding of how the spiritual gifts operate and grow in your confidence by using them. SEE 1 CORINTHIANS 14:1, 1 CORINTHIANS 12:1

Use Your Spiritual Gifts

You now have spiritual gifts!

Once you have received the overflowing power of the Holy Spirit you are able to begin function in or use the gifts that have been given to you. The word "gifts" in the bible is also translated "graces". They are spiritual expression of the presence of God within you. Paul says in 1 Corinthians 12:4-5 that

> *There are different kinds of gifts, but the same Spirit. There are different kinds of service, but the same Lord. There are different kinds of working, but the same God works all of them in all men*

Each believer has a combination of several spiritual gifts. As 1 Corinthians 12:7 says

> *Now to each one the manifestation of the Spirit is given for the common good*

They will greatly help your spiritual life. You need to know about your spiritual gifts because they help you grow in the supernatural realm and they help you God's will for your life.

So as Paul says in 1 Corinthians 12:1

> *Now about spiritual gifts, brothers, I do not want you to be ignorant*

Every believer received numerous spiritual gifts when you were born again and baptized in the Holy Spirit.

What Is a Spiritual Gift

A spiritual gift is a special grace or attribute given by the Holy Spirit to every spiritual son and daughter of God's family for use to demonstrate the kingdom of heaven here on earth now.

They are waiting for you to discover them and to use them to build God's kingdom here on earth.

They are received not earnt but they can be asked for by you. As 1 Corinthians 14:1 says

> *eagerly desire spiritual gifts*

Spiritual Gifts Are Not: -

Natural talents - They are super-natural! Spiritual gifts may or may not correspond to your natural talents.

Fruit of the Spirit - All Christians must produce fruit. Galatians 5:22-13 lists them as

> *"Love, joy peace, patience, kindness, goodness, faithfulness, gentleness and self-control."*

The fruit of the spirit describes what a Christian IS. Spiritual gifts define what a Christian DOES!

Spiritual gifts are not spiritual disciplines or roles of a Christian disciple such as prayer, fasting, giving, discipling and witnessing! Jesus said these should be practised by all believers regardless of your gifts!

You Need to Discover, Grow and Use Your Spiritual Gifts with The Support and Context of Other Believers.

See Appendix 2 for a list of the definition of Spiritual Gifts found in God's word.

CHAPTER 7

Glory That Lasts

Cindy Jacobs called my wife and I out in the middle of a meeting in Pasadena USA in June 2008 and prophesied that God wanted to pour out a spirit of revival on the geographical region that we were from in Southeast Queensland Australia.

It was a powerful word. When we shared it with our church back home God started an incredible hunger in us for revival in our city. Word spread quickly and soon there were seven churches who decided to start to pray together and hold a week of revival meetings.

After twenty-one days, God's presence in our meetings had increased dramatically and many people were healed and transformed.

That started a remarkable journey for us into the supernatural.

That opportunity is not limited to us. He has prompted us to tell you that you have an incredible opportunity right now! The Holy Spirit is drawing believers into a whole new level of glory experience. There are so many reports from around the world of spirit-led believers having whole new realms of Holy Spirit encounters.

But so many people don't realize how glorious His presence is!!!!

Their response is a lot like a woman's encounter with Jesus at a well in John 4. It tells us that Jesus asked a Samaritan woman for a drink of water. She objected because Jews didn't normally associate with Samaritans for religious reasons.

Jesus response to her was powerful and still speaks to us today. He said in John 4:10

> *If you knew the gift of God and who it is that asks you for a drink, you would have asked him and he would have given you living water.*

The "gift of God" was right in front of her but she could not "see" in the spirit or perceive the spirit realm. She did not have any spiritual perception. So she could have possibly missed out on the greatest spiritual encounter a person could ever experience.

For too long people have not understood how glorious God's presence is. Jesus put it this way in Matthew 5:6

> *Blessed are those who hunger and thirst for righteousness, for they will be filled*

When you are hungry and thirsty for the supernatural nothing will stop you. You crave His presence! So much so you thirst for spiritual living water!

The "Counterfeit" Of Satisfaction

One of the greatest challenges facing spiritual people is the "counterfeit of satisfaction." In its worst form it is religion!

What is religion?

It is where a person settles for the counterfeit of the real thing. It has an outward disguise of spirituality but it is empty. The danger is that every believer can end up settling for it.

Jesus hated religion. He criticized the religious more than anyone else. He called them hypocrites. He accused them in Matthew 23:25 of cleaning the outside but having self-indulgence on the inside.

So how does a person who loves the supernatural realm become religious?

The main thing that steals the substance of your supernatural encounter is the lack of His presence. It is allowing distractions and busyness to erode your intimacy with the Father. It results in you not taking time each day in God's presence!

This is the exact opposite to the way you grow in your spiritual encounter.

So you settle for the occasional drink of His glorious love instead of daily resting in Him! Eventually you only drink when you are with other believers.

But if they are doing the same, you settle for an outward form of something that once was!

It is a bit like eating 'out of date' chocolate. Maybe you are like me and there are days where I desire chocolate. Have you ever been in the situation late at night when you have wanted to eat some but there is none in your home.

One of my daughters is a preparatory school teacher. She teachers the very little children who are just starting school.

The great thing about being a "Prep" teacher is that the children regularly give their teachers gifts - often candy and chocolate.

So before my daughter was married she was a great source of late-night chocolate snacks.

On one occasion she didn't have her usual supply, and I had to resort to a piece she finally found that had melted and was very squashed and past it's used by date. A strange thing happened as I ate it. I knew it was chocolate so it was attractive and familiar, but it didn't taste quite right.

I felt the Holy Spirit say to me that it was just like religion. It has enough type of taste to draw us and even addict us even though there is something not quite right!

Worse still instead of admitting their need for living water, religion makes the same excuses as the woman at the well gave when she was confronted with her need to drink of the supernatural.

1st Excuse – Do what society expects of you.

In John 4:9

> The Samaritan woman said to him, "You are a Jew and I am a Samaritan woman. How can you ask me for a drink?" (For Jews do not associate

with Samaritans.)

We live in such a politically correct society, there is so much pressure for us to conform and fit in. There is continual pressure on you to adopt the world's values. But that is not who you are. You have chosen to be a supernatural person with a whole different set of priorities and values. If you want to live a supernatural lifestyle you must choose to please God first in your life.

2nd Excuse– Make practical reasons why you can't!

In John 4:11 the woman said to Jesus

> *Sir,...you have nothing to draw with and the well is deep*

The truth is that there will always be a practical reason why you cannot love a supernatural lifestyle. Natural reasoning will stop you from experiencing the supernatural. When you are truly thirsty nothing will stop you. Then you will move from relying on reason to being a person of wisdom!

3rd Excuse– Selfishness will always give you a way out.

In John 4:15 the woman said to Jesus

> "Sir, give me this water so that I won't get thirsty and have to keep coming here to draw water."

She was self-centered instead of being God-centered. They are the exact opposite! To encounter the realm of the supernatural you have to cross this bridge.

Selfishness is the main problem today in western society.

In fact it is the basis of all sins. Out of that comes greed, injustice, violence, poverty, oppression and all the other sins humans commit. It is why we need a Saviour in Jesus Christ. He is the only one who sets us free from this sin nature. Being self centered will stop your supernatural journey faster than an other thing. The supernatural requires us to move from us-centered to being Jesus-centered!

4th Excuse – Empty religious reasoning. In John 4:19-20 the woman said

> Sir, ...I can see that you are a prophet. Our fathers worshiped on this mountain, but you Jews claim that the place where we must worship is in Jerusalem.

Karl Marx declared that religion was the 'opiate of the masses'. (1)

While I believe Marx was wrong in the original context that he spoke this, there is an interesting context for glory absent religion.

Jesus hated religion because it caused people to look supernatural on the outside but have no real supernatural substance on the inside.

This is why he said in Matthew 23:27

> Woe to you, teachers of the law and Pharisees, you hypocrites! You are like whitewashed tombs, which look beautiful on the outside but on the inside are full of dead men's bones and everything unclean

That is what religion does. It drugs people like an opiate!

An opiate "dulls, blinds, desensitizes, but gives a sense of well-being." (2)

It even satisfies in a strange sort of way. But the most tragic thing for a believer who becomes religious is that they become sterile.

If you are sterile you are unable to reproduce!

That is why churches are more and more empty today.

They are unable to reproduce spiritual life and therefore become irrelevant.

All of these things steal what is God's original intention for you. Just like the woman at the well, the good news is that you too can break through into intimacy with God the Father through the love and sacrifice of His son Jesus the Christ.

As a result the supernatural glory becomes available to you as you grow in your understanding and experience of Him.

How To Access God's Supernatural Presence

What is glory?

The glory is the "manifest presence of God".

It is when the presence of God is shown plainly to you!

Without Christ you are excluded from the true supernatural realm.

In Ephesians 2:12 Paul explains it as being

> *...excluded from citizenship......... and foreigners to*

> *the covenants of the promise, without hope and without God in the world*

The reality is that the only lasting way you can experience the supernatural realm is by faith in Jesus Christ.

Paul describes it like this in Ephesians 2:13-14

> *But now in Christ Jesus you who once were far away have been brought near through the blood of Christ. For he himself is our peace, who has made the two one and has destroyed the barrier, the dividing wall of hostility*

He is not just speaking about your eternal salvation.

The cross is the window to heavenly glory!

Open the window and look with spiritual eyes.

This enables you to 'see' so you understand that God the Father has given you every access to the greatest supernatural encounter that a person can experience.

Paul said it best in Ephesians 1:3 that God has

> *blessed us in the heavenly realms with every spiritual blessing in Christ*

Wow!

What an opportunity!

The glory realm is wide open through Christ for you to step into.

When you understand the magnitude of this encounter you respond in the only possible way. And that is to praise

Him. The amazing thing is that the more we praise Him the more He opens the glory realm to us!

You are already seated with Christ in heavenly places! He has already given you full access into your heavenly supernatural encounter. You already have the capacity to live in the realm of the supernatural. Just believe it and step into it!

In John 3:13 Jesus lived in the earthly realm and heavenly realm at the same time.

So can you as sons of God! It says

> *No one has ever gone into heaven except the one who came from heaven — the Son of Man.*

So, our supernatural position is to do the same thing as Jesus did! We do that by stepping into it by faith. Jesus came to open the eyes of the blind. Allow him to open your blind eyes so you can 'see' supernaturally.

You can ascend and descend by faith into the supernatural realm.

Hebrews 9:24 says that this is a holy place that is not an earthly place but heaven itself.

> *For Christ did not enter a man-made sanctuary that was only a copy of the true one; he entered heaven itself, now to appear for us in God's presence*

We need to do it with confidence.

Hebrews 10:19-20 says we have confidence to enter the "holy place" into heavenly glory now.

How?

Therefore, brothers, since we have confidence to enter the Most Holy Place by the blood of Jesus, by a new and living way opened for us through the curtain, that is, his body

Glory That Fades

I often hear well-meaning Christians praying an old covenant prayer from Exodus 33:13-18 when Moses asked God to

'Now show me your glory'

Moses wanted God's presence to go with him.

Now that was a great insight and desire for that time!

But don't settle for second best because that is a glory that does not last!

Australia is part of the Commonwealth of Nations and Queen Elizabeth is our monarch.

When I was thirteen years old the Queen came to Australia to help celebrate our nations bicentenary. We heard that she was visiting our city and her official reception would be held in the sports stadium next to our school.

Our school decided that the students would line the streets to see her as she drove by. After waiting on the side of the road for what seemed like hours she finally approached. As she passed by, she turned her back to us and waved to those on the other side of the road.

I was so disappointed. My father rectified this late in the afternoon by finding out where we would be able to see her again as she drove to where she was staying for the evening.

As she approached, I started to run along the street wavering madly. So much so that I caught her attention and she smiled and waved at me.

Wow! I was on a mountain top of euphoria!

It took days for me to come back down to reality.

But eventually the glory of the experience wore off and it just became a faded boyhood memory.

In Exodus 34 we are told that when Moses encountered God's glory his face shone.

But 2 Corinthians 3:13 says his face shone only for a short time.

After he would come down from the mountain it faded.

I don't want to have a temporary fading supernatural experience. The good news is that you don't have to too.

Glory That Lasts

You can have the manifest presence of God that lasts! Let me show you.

In John 15:26 Jesus taught us to expect the Holy spirit to come to us personally so we could have the same glory that he had experienced! And this glory would not fade or go away.

Paul taught in 2 Corinthians 3:7-9 that

> *Now if the ministry that brought death, which was engraved in letters on stone, came with glory, so that the Israelites could not look steadily at the face of Moses because of its glory, fading though it was, will not the ministry of the Spirit be even more glorious? If the ministry that condemns men is glorious, how much more glorious is the ministry that brings righteousness!*

There is now a new Covenant between God and man. All we have to do is grab a hold of it through faith in the blood of Jesus Christ. So now you can have glory that remains!

Living In The Glory

Jesus gives us the key. We have to drink living water!

Jesus said in John 7:37

> *If any one is THIRSTY let HIM COME to ME and DRINK*

We must learn to be drinkers every day. Heidi Baker talks about learning how to get "snockered" in the Holy Spirit. (3)

She means to drink so much new wine of the spirit that you get your spirit man over-flowingly full. The more you drink the more you will overflow!

He says this in John 7:38

> *Whoever believes in me, as the Scripture has said, streams of living water will flow from within him*

You drink from the rivers of living water flowing up

inside of you. I tell you this works.

It is very hard to stay sad or depressed when you drinking living water.

It causes you to get happy! You get full of joy!

So much joy that it is running over.

For some reason this offends religious people. But I don't understand why you wouldn't want to get happy.

As the old song says "running over running over my cup is full and running over since the Lord saved me Im as happy as can be. My cup is full and running over."

The key is to drink living water every day until you overflow. The more you overflow with love and joy and peace then your life will start to affect others like never before.

This is what true bliss is.

Drink living water until you are drunk and let it overflow so it leaks onto others. You will open yourself up to whole new level of glory.

New Levels of Glory

One of the greatest revelations is that there are many levels of glory for us to experience.

Paul teaches us this way in 2 Corinthians 3:18

> *And we all, who with unveiled faces contemplate the Lord's glory, are being transformed into his image with ever increasing glory, which comes from the Lord, who is the Spirit*

The New Kings James version says we are changed "from glory to glory."

So as you encounter the supernatural, you can move from one level of glory to another.

Chapter 8 of Encountering the Supernatural deals specifically how to do this!

So instead of praying "Lord show us your Glory," we need to be praying, "Take me to the next level of Glory."

Glory Chasing with a Purpose

You were created for a divine purpose.

Psalms 139:16 says

> ...All the days ordained for me were written in your book before one of them came to be

Life is all about living your purpose. Not just any purpose. It is called a "divine destiny".

God says in Jeremiah 29:11

> For I know the plans I have for you," declares the LORD, "plans to prosper you and not to harm you, plans to give you hope and a future

To live your destiny you have to do something!

You have to position yourself for destiny.

My book "Fathering a Destiny" teaches you how to do just that! (4)

The truth is you need to boldly do the things that define

you. 2 Corinthians 3:12

> *Therefore since we have this hope WE ARE VERY BOLD!*

The leader of the largest church in the world Dr. Yonghi Cho says "We have enough Holy Spirit. We must boldly use what we have inside us and be bold!" (5)

Step Boldly Into the Next Level of Glory for You

Paul understood this. He taught to only chase the glory that lasts.

In 2 Corinthians 3:16 -17, he said that the old understanding is taken away and instead God's surpassing glory is available for us that results in more and more freedom. Freedom that moves us to the next level of glory!

You need to decide to step boldly into your next level. Then we can live in increasing levels of glory!

PRAY WITH ME

Why don't you pray with me right now to experience exactly what I have been writing about.

"Jesus I ask for a revelation about the true state of my spiritual life. Expose the religious excuses. I choose to step in to the freedom and power of God's glory. Transform me from glory to glory. Show me the things that steal from the glory flowing in my life. I decide to step up into the next level of glory in Jesus name."

CHAPTER 8

Moving To The Next Level Of The Supernatural

A friend of mine tells of the first time she experienced supernatural travel. She was flying on a plane to Africa to minister in a region where she hadn't been before.

She knew she would have to confront a difficult situation once she arrived. She prayed as she looked out the window. Suddenly she was no longer in the plane but looking over the region she was travelling to. She still had many hours of flight left but in the Holy Spirit she was already there.

She prayed strategically for the problem, and the Lord spoke to her about how to handle the situation.

Then just as suddenly she was back in her airplane seat.

Amazingly over an hour had past but it felt like just a few minutes.

When she finally did arrive at her destination the next day she recognized the leaders even though they had never met before. When they discussed the problem, they told her that things had dramatically changed the day before at the same time that she had been there praying in the spirit!

Next Level

You can easily move to your next level of encountering the supernatural. In fact the Bible teaches that you are not supposed to stay at the level of supernatural encounter that you are now.

Paul is very clear in his second letter the Corinthian believers and to you. In Chapter 3 he clearly shows that you are under a new spirit of freedom that allows us to move from one level of glory to another. You do not have to be like Moses who covered his face with a veil when he experienced God's glory.

In 2 Corinthians 3:18 he says

> *"But we all, with unveiled face, beholding as in a mirror the glory of the Lord, are being transformed into the same image from glory to glory, just as by the Spirit of the Lord."* (NKJV)

So you are able to experience God's glory (His supernatural presence) now! As well you can move from one level of glory to another.

The Bible does describe five different levels of glory that all can experience. The goal must be to go from one level of glory to another.

1st Level - Created In God's Image

We are all created in the image of God so therefore we all have first level of Glory.

Genesis 1:27 says

> *So God created man in his own image, in the image of God he created him; male and female he created them*

Humanity is the entry level of glory. You all experience this level of glory.

John Crowder explains in his book 'The Ecstasy of Loving God'. He says that you all use this level of glory when you pray.

Typically, your mind is flooded with thoughts and memories and things you have to do when you first try to pray.

The key is do not try and make those thoughts go away. They are not distractions but the first level of Glory in operation in your life. The Holy Spirit is enabling you to recall the things that need to be handed over to Jesus.

The way to do that is to cast or role your cares over to him. Jesus is the burden bearer.

1 Peter 5:7 says to cast your cares on the Lord.

The actual Greek meaning of this term "cast" is to "lift up & roll over onto your burden bearer"

James 4:7 tells the result of doing this!

You draw near to God and He draws near to you. So the more you understand the function of the first level of glory, you draw closer to God. So close that you move to the second level of glory!

2nd Level - Baptized In His Glory

The second level of glory is experienced when you are born again.

John 3:3 says

> No one can SEE the kingdom of God unless he is born again

Verse 5 speaks of every person being able to be born of the spirit. When you are born again you enter the kingdom of God and the Kingdom of God enters you.

From that time forward "the kingdom of Heaven is within you". God's supernatural presence dwells in your regenerated spirit man.

The Bible also described how to be baptized into His Holy Spirit! As explained in detail in Chapter 6 this is an additional experience to being born again.

Acts 8 tells about how the apostles in Jerusalem had heard that people in Samaria had accepted the gospel. So they sent Peter and John to help them.

In Acts 8:15-17 we see that

> When they arrived, they prayed for them that they might receive the Holy Spirit, because the Holy Spirit had not yet come upon any of them;

they had simply been baptized into the name of the Lord

Jesus. Then Peter and John placed their hands on them, and they received the Holy Spirit

The word "baptism" means to immerse or dunk. Father God wants to immerse you or baptize you with His glory!

Romans 8: 14-17 tells us how this causes you to "share in his glory."

Why don't you find a believer who has been baptized in the Holy Spirit and ask them to lay hands on you and pray you experience the same thing.

When you do this, the Holy Spirit will speak to you personally and then He starts working in us and through us to help others.

One of the first times this happened to me was in the city mall in the center of my hometown. I was a part of an outreach team of twenty people that had gone in the city on a Saturday night to share God's love to others. We began by singing worship songs in a circle.

We worshipped until the presence of God (His supernatural glory) filled us to overflowing. Quite a crowd had gathered to watch us and we turned to speak to them. As I approached a young man, I heard the Holy Spirit say "He has just broken up with is girlfriend and he is so heartbroken that he has decided to kill himself." After I introduced myself, I proceeded to tell him what I just heard about him. He was astounded. And I was able to pray for him. He left a very different person.

3rd Level - Intimacy Of The Father

Becoming a son (or daughter) of the Father is the entry point to true intimacy. You can't be led into greater levels of glory until you learn to be a child of God.

Romans 8:14 (b) says

> *because those who are led by the Spirit of God are sons of God*

Paul goes on to say that it is possible to receive a "spirit of sonship". In my first book "Fathering a destiny - Growing spiritual sons and daughters" I share my own personal journey of being set free from an orphan spirit and discovering God as a loving personal father for the first time. The result has been incredible intimacy with the father.

Intimacy leads to greater passion and holiness and the next level of glory. It is where the presence of God is present ALL the time.

I've heard it said that holiness is not the absence of sin but the presence of God. A lot of the traditional religions practice meditation by emptying themselves of all their consciousness. My response is that does not draw you closer to God. Rather when you empty yourselves of sin you are still empty.

Don't get empty, instead get full!

Get full of God's supernatural glory.

When the adopted children at Heidi Bakers Church in Mozambique prayed for me I got adopted and lost my orphan spirit forever.

The spirit of sonship causes you to experience the intimacy of knowing Papa God. A wonderful friend of mine refers to this as her daily "Yummy Daddy Time!"

As Romans 8:17 says

> Now if we are children, then we are heirs—heirs of God and co-heirs with Christ, if indeed we share in his sufferings in order that we may also share in his glory

Other people start to recognize heart of Father God in you.

It is no longer about you or your ministry. Now it is about being found in Him.

4th Level - Union

All these levels of God's supernatural glory are available for you to experience. Each one is dependent on the other.

Union is the fourth level of glory. Union is where two separate beings become one. This great experience is called a "mystery" by the Apostle Paul in Ephesians 5. You get an insight into this through the picture of the "union of marriage." Paul describes the incredible power of Christ's love for us (his bride the church) when He "gave himself up for her" so he could make her holy so she (us) would be "cleansed "to such an extent that she would be perfect - "without stain, wrinkle or blemish."

Then he declares in Ephesians 5:31-32

> *After all, no one ever hated his own body, but he feeds and cares for it, just as Christ does the church— for we are members of his body. "For this reason a man will leave his father and mother and be united to his wife, and the two will become one flesh." This is a profound mystery—but I am talking about Christ and the church.*

This verse is often quoted at weddings. But it is not just talking about marriage between a man and a woman. There is a greater union to be experienced here.

To enter this fourth level of glory means to be union with Jesus.

So you become absorbed by Him. It is the place of being totally overwhelmed by the Greater Glory of just being WITH HIM! You are undone in His presence.

Paul helps to explain the meaning of level of glory when he shares in Galatians 2:20 of dying to your 'self-life' and allowing Christ to live through you. This is not intellectual understanding of dying to self but the spiritual experience of dying to self once and for all and allowing only Christ living in you.

This level of glory is also the realm where supernatural occurrences begin to happen with great frequency. The realm of the supernatural becomes common place.

Intimate union with Him is the priority above all all else. But the overflow is the realm of trances, dreams and out of body experiences such as translocation. All of these things are found in the Bible.

These were experienced by the people in the early church, the mystics, and even Christians today who understand the supernatural glory of God!

For example, in Acts 8:39-40 Philip was physically taken by the Holy Spirit to another region. This is called bi-location and does happen to believers today who know how to move into this level of glory.

The mistake is that people seek the supernatural manifestations and not union with Him. You cannot have them without the union.

Lou Engle, the founder of The Call prayer movement teaches about receiving insight and answers through what he calls the "The Dream Stream". Since Lou prayed for me, God often speaks to me very clearly through spiritual dreams often as much as two or three times a week. What is happening? The level of supernatural glory is manifesting itself through my subconscious as I sleep. There are many examples of directional dreams in the Bible. It was Peter on the Day of Pentecost that declared in Acts 2:17

> *In the last days, God says, I will pour out my Spirit on all people. Your sons and daughters will prophesy, your young men will see visions, your old men will dream dreams*

I experienced a vision when I was in Israel for the The Call Jerusalem in May 2008. The Call was a solemn assembly according to Joel 2:15-16.

It involved twelve hours of corporate prayer and fasting with thousands of believers from all around the world. After five hours of prayer, I entered a trance. I saw a lion that had been asleep that began to wake up!

In the trance I asked the Lord what does that mean?

He said "That lion is you. You have been asleep too long. It is time to wake up and roar for your nation."

When I came out of the trance I was undone. I spent many hours weeping and repenting before God. My life changed that day.

I have seen Cindy Jacobs go into a trance while she was speaking publicly last year. One minute she is speaking with power. The next she fell limply on the floor where she stayed for over an hour. The following night she told how she had gone to heaven in a trance for over an hour.

A missionary friend has spent many decades ministering in Bougainville in the South Pacific. They tell the story of a group of Christian leaders last decade who were burdened by the large number of suicides murders and unexplained deaths among their friends and family on a neighboring island. They decided that it must change and so they spent the entire night praying. Suddenly they were physically on the other island. Even though they had no natural knowledge of the whereabouts, they were led to a certain location where they started to dig. Immediately they uncovered human bones in a witchcraft formation. They removed the bones and supernaturally found themselves back in their original prayer circle. From that date forward there were subsequently no unusual deaths or murders.

While these types of experiences are exciting and cause many believers to be hungry to also want to experience the same things. Remember this level of supernatural glory comes from your union with Jesus Christ. It is yours to be entered into through intimacy.

5th Level - Ecstatic

This is the level of Ecstatic! This is the "surpassing glory" that Paul is referring to in 2 Corinthians 3:10.

> *"For what was glorious has no glory now in comparison with the surpassing glory"*

The realm of Ecstatic or Ecstasy is literally heavenly! It is the momentary lose self of control where you literally are there in heaven. It is the speechless state of being in the presence of God. Those who have this experience are never the same. They have been to taken into heaven and the lives have been eternally impacted!

John Crowder calls it the "Consistent state of tangible ecstatic communion with God" (1)

It is called bilocation. Paul spoke about a person being caught up into the third heaven.

In 2 Corinthians 12:2

> *"I know a man in Christ who fourteen years ago*

was caught up to the third heaven. Whether it was in the body or out of the body I do not know—God knows."

So, it is possible for you to experience this realm too!

But there is a interesting sequel. It is not just about having a once off heavenly experience. For it possible to live in "a constant awareness of the presence of God." It is possible to live there by faith and go there at will!

Ecstasy also is called "bliss". It is where you live in the continual love, joy, peace and "bliss" of God. Ecstasy is where you live in heavenly realm here on earth. So it is much more than a trip to heaven! It is the bliss of supernatural glory here on earth right now! And it is available to you too!

Hebrews 9:24 show us that the holy place is not earthy man made place in a temple but heaven itself.

Hebrews 10:19 tells us we can have confidence to enter the "holy place" of heaven. How? Through the blood of Christ. And you can ascend and descend in this realm by faith.

> *Therefore, brothers, since we have confidence to enter the Most Holy Place by the blood of Jesus, by a new and living way opened for us through the curtain, that is, his body, and since we have a great priest over the house of God, let us draw near to God with a sincere heart in full assurance of faith, having our hearts sprinkled to cleanse us from a guilty conscience and having our bodies washed with pure water*

The Whole Purpose

The whole purpose of going deeper into greater levels of glory is to draw nearer and nearer to God. He is the lover of your souls. The true reason for the existence of human kind is to know God's love and to make His love known.

The truth is His love is out of this world. He is the one demonstrated His ultimate love on a cross so you and I are free to love and live. The ecstatic is the culmination of the pursuit of God in return for this amazing love demonstration. A love so great that when you experience it takes you to another realm.

Kathryn Kulhman describes it this way.

"And when he touches me, I can go for a long time and not be conscious of another single person. I am only conscious of His presence and of following Him. I am a violin played by a master violinist. It is like waves of glory almost lifting me out of my body. The Spirit touches the strings of my heart and plays beautiful music." (2)

When Kathryn Ruonala was a child she became very upset because she wanted to see "Jesus face". She asked for Jesus to show her his face. Today she has an amazing ministry of prophetic healing and evangelism. Her secret? Intimacy! She says the more she looks into Jesus face, the more miracles happen! (3)

The truth is that you reflect what you behold. The more you seek His face the more you will live in His glory. The more you seek Him the more you become like Him!

The best example of this is Stephen in Acts 7:55-56

> ...Stephen, full of the Holy Spirit, looked up to heaven and saw the glory of God, and Jesus standing at the right hand of God. "Look," he said, "I see heaven open and the Son of Man standing at the right hand of God."

The way into the glory is the intimacy with the Father. The more you experience it the more you desire it!

It comes and is experienced through daily dependency intimacy, communion and revelation of the ecstasy of God. It is yours too!

Today decide to move from your current of glory to the next!

CHAPTER 9

Your Supernatural Transformation

Congratulations. As you have read this book you have already progressed in your encounter into the supernatural. It will continue to develop from now on too.

Everyone is a different place in their encounter, so it is very important that you do not compare your progress with others. What is important is the realisation that you can progress in your supernatural transformation every day.

The supernatural transformation process in your life is identical to the metamorphose process that takes place in nature. The good news is that your are continually being transformed in to the supernatural person you were created by God to become.

Metamorphose is wonderful process in nature. God even uses that word in original Greek meaning on the word "transformed" in Romans 12:2

> *Do not conform any longer to the pattern of this world, but be transformed (metamorphosed) by*

the renewing of your mind.

Biologically the "metamorphosis" process is defined as a "profound change in form from one stage to the next in the life history of an organism," as from the caterpillar to the pupa and from the pupa to the adult butterfly."

So why cant we also experience that same profound change in our substance so we are transformed from a natural to supernatural person.

Romans 12:2 goes on to say that this pleases God because

> *Then you will be able to test and approve what God's will is—his good, pleasing and perfect will.*

Encounters That Transform You For Life

When God moves with His glory your life is never the same! It does not matter what any other person says, you know your life has changed.

When an angel of the Lord show up! The truth is whether you are a believer or an atheist when the supernatural takes place you will quake!

Just imagine with me the resurrection of Jesus from the perspective of the soldiers guarding Jesus's tomb!

Matthew 28: 2 - 4 tells us that

> *There was a violent earthquake, for an angel of the Lord came down from heaven and, going to the tomb, rolled back the stone and sat on it.*

His appearance was like lightning, and his clothes were white as snow.

The guards were so afraid of him that they shook and became like dead men

Can you see it? The soldiers are on guard and then suddenly an angel appears and God's presence knocked them out. They lay on the ground quaking with fear.

Imagine many years later they are relating this event to their grandchildren.

Even though they were later bribed by the religious hypocrites to say that the resurrection did not happen, what they supernaturally encountered impacted them for life!

Why? Because instantly they knew Jesus was who people said he was! They had a transformation encounter that moved them into the supernatural realm.

One of our friends has a great healing gift. So far this year over one hundred and fifty people have had a supernatural born again encounter with Jesus after they or a family member were dramatically healed. Why? They saw and believed!

Two friends of mine recently went to the intensive care unit in a hospital in our city to pray for a man who was dying of a ruptured oesophagus. His body was full of infection. He was in a coma with only hours left to live. The rupture had resulted in contamination of his lungs and other organs. My friends anointed him with oil, prayed for him declaring healing with the authority of Christ's word. This was done twenty minutes before he was scheduled for emergency surgery by a specialist surgeon to try to repair the rupture as a last resort. When the surgeon carefully examined the oesophagus he could not find any rupture at all. They were dumbfounded. Instead of taking another four months to recover as predicted he was made a remarkable recovery in the past two weeks. The nurses and the doctors refer to this event as a miracle as there was no evidence of the previous rupture. They have encountered the supernatural and has caused them to think differently. That is what the supernatural is supposed to do to us!

The classic example of a supernatural encounter changing the way a person thinks is found Acts 9. In begins in verse 1 by telling us that

> Saul was still breathing out murderous threats against the Lord's disciples. He went to the high priest and asked him for letters to the synagogues in Damascus, so that if he found any there who belonged to the Way, whether men or women, he might take them as prisoners to Jerusalem.

He was intent on continuing to arrest and even murdering the Christians! But then he encountered the supernatural!

Acts 9: 3-4 tells us that

> As he neared Damascus on his journey, suddenly a light from heaven flashed around him. He fell to the ground and heard a voice say to him, "Saul, Saul, why do you persecute me?

How would you have responded to a supernatural light

from heaven flashing around you and then you hear a voice from heaven?

I guarantee that you would never be the same too! It is called instant transformation!

I was also true for Jesus encounter at the mount of transfiguration. Matthew 17:1- 3 there was also a light and then in verse 5 tells us there was a voice from heaven too!

> *While he was still speaking, a bright cloud enveloped them, and a voice from the cloud said, "This is my Son, whom I love; with him I am well pleased. Listen to him!"*

Transformation encounters cause you to see the light! You see things differently from then on. Your mind is opened up to hear the voice of the Holy Spirit so you are never the same.

This transformation by supernatural encounter was also true for Moses's supernatural encounter. God's presence would physically envelop Moses each time he went into the Tent of Meeting to speak to God "as a man would speak to a friend."

When Moses wanted to take his encounter further he said to God in Exodus 33:18 "Show me your glory."

God's response in Exodus 33:19 was that

> *I will cause all my goodness to pass in front of you, and I will proclaim my name, the LORD, in your presence. I will have mercy on whom I will*

> have mercy, and I will have compassion on whom I will have compassion. This gives an insight into what God's supernatural transformational does and is! It is only does you good as it is full of God's goodness and His manifest presence.

It is so powerful that Moses had to hide his face in a crevasse of a rock. He couldn't look at God's face and physically stand it! In face you are unable to look at God's face and live!

This makes a mockery of the statement "if you show me God I will believe" doesn't it? The truth is you won't, you'll just die!

The bottom line when you step into the realm of supernatural transformation that you will never be the same again! And why would you want to be same!

You will join with Patricia King who says, "Miracles happen every day to me!" (1)

That is how I want to live. And miracles will happen to you when you live daily in the supernatural!

How Do You Live In The Supernatural?

And for the bottom line! How do you live (not just visit there once or twice in your life) in the supernatural?

Jesus gives us the key in John 7:37. We have to drink living water!

> *If any one is THIRSTY let him COME to ME and DRINK*

The question is how thirsty are you?

You have to learn to drink every day.

Heidi Baker says that you need to get drunk in the Holy Ghost every day.

In other words you drink so much new wine of the spirit that you get your spirit man gets over flowingly full.

The more you drink the more you will overflow!

Jesus said in John 7:38

> *Whoever believes in me, as the Scripture has said, streams of living water will flow from within him.*

You drink from the rivers of living water flowing up inside of you.

I tell you this works.

It is very hard to stay sad or depressed when you drinking living water.

It causes you to get happy!

You get full of joy! So much joy that it is running over.

For some reason this offends religious people. I don't understand why you wouldn't want to get happy?

This is not something new! This has been the case from the time of Jesus.

There are even old songs that are hundreds of years old that prove this.

Songs like

Running over running over my cup is full and running

ever since the Lord saved me I'm as happy as can be. My cup is full and running over.

The key is to drink living water every day until you overflow. The more you overflow with love and joy and peace then your life will start to affect others like never before.

A good friend from Canada shares about how one new Christian had a dramatic experience in on their chat room on the internet one night recently.

This young man was talking to a girl in Australia who was having major problems paying her rent. So much so she was about to be evicted later in the week. As they were speaking his friend had a supernatural encounter.

He saw in the spirit realm. It was a bookshelf in a room and on the shelf was a brown bible and he saw a specific page number.

He asked the woman online on the other side of the world if she had a brown bible on her bookshelf. The woman said that she did. It was a gift from her grandfather who had recently passed away. He told her to go and get the bible and turn that specific page. As she did this she screamed!

At that exact page was an envelope containing the exact amount of money she needed to pay her rent that week!

How did he know?

The supernatural transformation in him by Jesus overflowed over into her exact need. It transformed her life. She became a follower of Jesus too!

This Is What Supernatural Transformation Is Like

You are transformed for others!

This is not about you!

The gospel has always been about loving God and loving others!

But if you are not encountering living water daily you have nothing to share spiritually with others. If you drink living water until you are drunk and let it overflow so it leaks on others then you will open yourself up to whole new level of glory. Where there is glory there is transformation!

Gary had an injury in his leg for twenty years. One day he and his wife went to a Christian meeting and were so impacted by the power of the Holy Spirit that they came home drunk in the Holy Spirit. As they continued to worship Jesus in their lounge room, Gary's wife leant across and placed her hand on his sore leg. The power of that encounter knocked him off his feet. The next day Gary rose early and went for a long walk on the beach with his friend. When he arrived home his wife asked him how was his leg? He suddenly realized that he had no pain all day. His leg was completely healed and has been perfect since. What happened the supernatural overflow of joy and power transformed him physically!

The apostles relied on the supernatural transformation of God! Paul says in 2 Corinthians 3:2-3

> *You yourselves are our letter, written on our hearts, known and read by everybody. You show*

that you are a letter from Christ, the result of our ministry, written not with ink but with the Spirit of the living God, not on tablets of stone but on tablets of human hearts.

They were transformed to transform others' lives! So must we!

Our Supernatural Mandate

God's supernatural ways are limitless. His supernatural kingdom is always working even when our natural eyes cannot see it!

In other words, the supernatural is ALWAYS at work whether we can see it or not! The main purpose of supernatural transformation is to participate in for the sake of the supernatural transformation of others!

You have a supernatural mandate. It is to "Let God's people go!"

In the second book of the bible, the book of Exodus tells the story of God raising up a deliverer for the God's chosen people who were in slavery in Egypt. His name was Moses. They have even made a movie about this called the Prince of Egypt.

You can read the story in Exodus 3-12.

Repeatedly Moses said the words of God to Pharaoh "Let my people go"!

Pharaoh represents the skeptical attitude and logic of western society that I spoke of in the Introduction to this book!

God is saying again "Let my people go! Let my people go so they can experience my supernatural freedom and transformation and take it to others".

Let them go to their friends, neighbors, family members and any person who has genuine hunger for more to life than what they are experiencing!

For too long God's people have had this back to front!

Jesus went to the people and performed miracles! He did not wait for the people to come to him in a building! The people only followed him AFTER they encountered him and His miracles! Your supernatural mandate is to go and do the same!

DECLARATION

"My prayer for you is that you will so encounter the supernatural that you will life will never be the same. Holy Spirit I ask that you come with power on person reading this book. That they would so encounter you that you would transform them into someone who sees and lives in the supernatural realm. So much so that others will be transformed by the overflow of your presence coming out of them in Jesus name!"

Appendix 1

Key Healing References in the Bible

Exodus 15:26

> "He said, "If you listen carefully to the voice of the LORD your God and do what is right in his eyes, if you pay attention to his commands and keep all his decrees, I will not bring on you any of the diseases I brought on the Egyptians, for I am the LORD, who heals you."

Exodus 23:25

> "Worship the LORD your God, and his blessing will be on your food and water. I will take away sickness from among you.."

Psalm 103:2-3

> "Praise the LORD, O my soul, and forget not all his benefits— who forgives all your sins and heals all your diseases"

Psalm 107:20

> "He sent forth his word and healed them..."

Isaiah 53:5

> "But he was pierced for our transgressions, he was crushed for our iniquities; the punishment that brought us peace was upon him, and by his wounds we are healed."

Malachi 4:2

> "But for you who revere my name, the sun of righteousness will rise with healing in its wings.."

Matthew 8: 16-17

> "When evening came, many who were demon-possessed were brought to him, and he drove out the spirits with a word and healed all the sick. This was to fulfill what was spoken through the prophet Isaiah: "He took up our infirmities and carried our diseases."

Mark 16:17-18

> "And these signs will accompany those who believe: In my name they will drive out demons; they will speak in new tongues; they will pick up snakes with their hands; and when they drink deadly poison, it will not hurt them at all; they will place their hands on sick people, and they will get well."

Luke 13:16

> "Then should not this woman, a daughter of

APPENDIX 1

> *Abraham, whom Satan has kept bound for eighteen long years, be set free on the Sabbath day from what bound her."*

Acts 10:38

> *"...how God anointed Jesus of Nazareth with the Holy Spirit and power, and how he went around doing good and healing ALL who were under the power of the devil, because God was with him."*
>
> *(Uppercase added)*

James 5:14-15

> *"Is any one of you sick? He should call the elders of the church to pray over him and anoint him with oil in the name of the Lord. And the prayer offered in faith will make the sick person well; the Lord will raise him up. If he has sinned, he will be forgiven."*

James 5:16

> *"Therefore confess your sins to each other and pray for each other so that you may be healed..."*

1 Peter 2:24

> *"He himself bore our sins in his body on the tree, so that we might die to sins and live for righteousness; by his wounds YOU HAVE BEEN healed."*
>
> *(Uppercase added)*

3 John 2

"I pray that you may enjoy good health and that all may go well with you, even as your soul is getting along well."

Appendix 2

Definitions Of Spiritual Gifts

as listed in 1 Corinthians 12:4-10, Romans 12:6-8

PROPHECY

The gift of prophecy is the special ability that God gives to His spiritual sons and daughters to speak forth by direct inspiration of the Holy Spirit the words of God to his people.

EVANGELISM

The gift of evangelist is the special ability that God gives to His spiritual sons and daughters to share the good news of salvation with unbelievers in such an effective way that people become Jesus' disciples and members of His family.

PASTORING

The gift of pastoring is the special ability that God gives to His spiritual sons and daughters to personally love, teach and inspire a group of believers over a long period of time.

TEACHING

The gift of teaching is the special ability that God gives to His spiritual sons and daughters to mentor, correct, instruct and impart truth to believers in such a way that they grow up in their faith.

FAITH

The gift of faith is the special ability that God gives to His spiritual sons and daughters to discern with extraordinary confidence that God will do what He has promised. It is a supernatural confidence for a specific situation that what they are believing for will become a reality.

TONGUES FOR PUBLIC WORSHIP

The gift of tongues is the special ability that God gives to His spiritual sons and daughters to communicate a message from God in a language they have never learned in a public worship setting.

TONGUES AS PERSONAL PRAYER LANGUAGE

The gift of tongues as a personal prayer language is the special ability that God gives to pray in a language they have never learned. This gift edifies the person who prays and causes them to be spiritually sensitive to the voice of the Holy Spirit

MIRACLES

The gift of miracles the special ability that God gives to His spiritual sons and daughters to bring about a supernatural intervention on the ordinary course of nature by the Spirit of God

HEALING

The gift of healing is the special ability that God gives to

His spiritual sons and daughters through whom God uses to supernaturally give health and healing to others who are sick.

INTERPRETATION OF TONGUES

The gift of interpretation of tongues is the special ability that God gives to His spiritual sons and daughters to interpret a message that has been given in tongues in a public place of worship.

WORD OF KNOWLEDGE

The word of knowledge is special ability God gives to His spiritual sons and daughters to supernaturally know information about others that they would not naturally know. Specifically this is used in conjunction with the gift of Healing to physically heal others, the gift of the Word of Wisdom and the gift of Encouragement.

WORD OF WISDOM

A word of wisdom is special ability God gives to His spiritual sons and daughters to supernaturally give specific solutions for specific needs in others lives.

DISCERNING OF SPIRITS

The gift of discerning of spirits is the supernatural ability given by the Holy Spirit to His spiritual sons and daughters to discern the difference between the Holy Spirit, demons and soul issues. This gift typically can discern when someone is not telling the truth.

ENCOURAGEMENT

The gift of encouragement is the special ability that God

gives to His spiritual sons and daughters to give encouragement and wise advice to people in such a way that their stress is alleviated and they see a solution to their circumstance.

LEADERSHIP

The gift of leadership is the special ability that God gives to His spiritual sons and daughters to discern God's purpose for the future and to clearly communicate this to others in such a way that causes them follow a common purpose in the spirit of unity.

ADMINISTRATION

The gift of administration is the special ability that God gives to His spiritual sons and daughters to organise, oversee and implement effective plans for the common good of a wider group of people.

HOSPITALITY

The gift of hospitality is the special ability that God gives to His spiritual sons and daughters to make others feel welcome and honoured in such a way that they feel accepted, valued and at home.

INTERCESSION

The gift of intercession is the special ability that God gives to His spiritual sons and daughters to pray consistently and regularly for specific spiritual, national and practical needs. Intercessors know that intercession practically and spiritually changes circumstances, lives, cities and even governments. So intercession becomes the priority.

GIVING

The gift of giving is the special ability that God gives to His spiritual sons and daughters to attract and give finances and other resources to build the kingdom of God here on earth

MERCY

The gift of mercy is the special ability that God gives to His spiritual sons and daughters to feel genuine love and compassion for all who are suffering or in distress.

HELPS

The gift of helps is the special ability that God gives to His spiritual sons and daughters to effectively use many practical talents they have to help those with other gifts be more productive in their spiritual gifts

SERVICE

The gift of service is the special ability that God gives to His spiritual sons and daughters to identify and meet the needs in spiritual organisations and help accomplish those specific goals.

MISSIONARY

The gift of missionary is the special ability that God gives to His spiritual sons and daughters to use their spiritual gifts they have in a cross cultural setting.

MUSIC

The gift of music is the special ability that God gives to to build up and encourage and His spiritual sons and daughters lead other believers into God's presence through music and accompanying songs.

CRAFTSMANSHIP

The gift of craftsmanship is the special ability that God gives to His spiritual sons and daughters to design, and build items that are especially used to worship God.

CELIBACY

The gift of celibacy is the special ability that God gives to His spiritual sons and daughters remain single, self controlled in sexual desires and happy not to marry.

MARTYRDOM

The gift of martyrdom is the special ability that God gives to His spiritual sons and daughters who willingly suffer and even to die for their faith in joyful attitude of victory for Christ.

ENDNOTES

Introduction

(1) Todd and DeAnn Burke - 'Anointed for Burial - God's faithfulness and miracles in the midst of Cambodia's darkest hour'. Published 1977 by Bridge Logos Publishers

Chapter 1

(1) Hymn - 'And Can It Be that I Should Gain' Words: Charles Wesley, 1739 Music: Thomas Campbell, 1835

Chapter 3

(1) Ralph Wilkerson - 'Kathryn Kuhlman's Healing Words' From the library of Ralph Wilkerson. Published by Charisma House Page 40

Chapter 4

(1) Owen Jorgensen - 'Supernatural: The Life of William Branham, Book Four: The Evangelist and His Acclamation (1951-1954) (Book 4) Self-published 2001

(2) Kathryn Kuhlman - 'I believe in Miracles' Volume 1 - The Kathryn Kuhlman Foundation www.kathrynkuhlman.com/products.html

Chapter 5

(1)   Gordon Lindsay - 'William Branham - A man sent from God' Published by William Branham, Jeffersonville, Indiana

(2)   Kevin Dedmon - 'The Ultimate Treasure Hunt: A guide to supernatural evangelism through supernatural encounters' Published by Bethel, Redding California

Chapter 6

(1)   Stanley Frodsham - 'Smith Wigglesworth: Apostle of Faith" Published 1993 by Gospel Publishing House

(2)   Bruce Lindley - 'Fathering a Destiny - Growing Spiritual Sons and Daughters'

Published by Faith Builders International, Robina, Queensland

(3)   Derek Prince - 'They Shall Expel Demons: What You Need to Know about Demons Your Invisible Enemies' Published 1998 by Chosen Books

Chapter 7

(1)   Karl Marx - 'Critique of Hegel's Philosophy of Right' Published in 1977 by Cambridge University Press (first published 1843)

(2)   Dictionary.com, LLC. Copyright © 2011. All rights reserved

(3)   Heidi Baker - Iris Ministries www.irisminstries.org

(4)   Dr. Yonghi Cho - 'The Fourth Dimension' Volume 1 Published in 1979 Logos International

ENDNOTES

Chapter 8

(1)	John Crowder - 'The Esctacy of Loving God'. Published in 2009 by Destiny Image

(2)	Ralph Wilkerson - 'Kathryn Kuhlman's Healing Words' from the library of Ralph Wilkerson. Published by Charisma House Page 40 -41

(3)	Katherine Ruonala - 'Make Room for God' - Audio Series. Available at New Day Ministries www.newdayministries.org.au

(4)	Bruce Lindley - 'Fathering a Destiny - Growing Spiritual Sons and Daughters' Published by Faith Builders International, Robina, Queensland

Chapter 9

(1)	Patricia King - 'Growing in the Supernatural' - Cd series. Available at Extreme Prophetic www.xpmedia.com

ARC Global Apostolic Community

ARC Global is a new apostolic community of apostles and prophets who are committed to building Godly community, through love, encouragement, equipping others for growth, and next generational legacy.

On 8th November 2013 ARC Global was launched by the Holy Spirit in the presence of our Apostolic Community of apostles, prophets & watchmen to the nations. We believe a whole new level of international apostolic authority & apostolic influence has been released! To God be the Glory.

ARC Global is not a denomination or a hierarchy of people in authority. It is a network based on relationships not 'position' or 'title'. It is a new wineskin that embraces all those who share the calling to transform society.

ARC Global is committed to:-

Help you grow into the fullness of your God mandate through apostolic community

Walk together in strategic relationships in community

Build the kingdom of God together

Equip & send Apostolic & Prophetic teams in Australia & the nations

Establish houses of prayer in Australia & the nations

Network together to transform nations

Father next Generation of emerging apostles & prophets

Connect like hearted like-minded leaders in Community

To connect to ARC Global see ***www.arcglobal.org***

Bruce Lindley's Other Books And Resources

1. 'Fathering a Destiny - Growing Spiritual Sons and Daughters'

   A great leadership book that will help you discover your God destiny and grow the destiny of others. You will learn how to position in your destiny.

2. 'The Father's Love - An Encounter with God the Father' - A workbook that will help you encounter the Father heart of God

3. 'The Seeing Transformation' - Foreword by Patricia King - If you change the way you SEE, everything will change!

4. A Whole New Era - Emerging Apostles & Prophets Today' - Foreword by Che Ahn - For all apostles & prophets & those wanting to grow into their 5fold office.

5. 'Longevity in Leadership – How to Run the Race and Finish Well'

To order visit Amazon

To contact Bruce Lindley to arrange speaking engagements or additional resources email: *admin@arcglobal.org*

www.ingramcontent.com/pod-product-compliance
Lightning Source LLC
Chambersburg PA
CBHW051439290426
44109CB00016B/1621